THOUGHT CATALOG BOOKS

Tell the Truth, Let the Peace Fall Where it May

Tell the Truth, Let the Peace Fall Where it May

How Authentic Living Creates the Passion, Fulfillment & Love You Seek

BRYAN REEVES

THOUGHT CATALOG BOOKS

Brooklyn, NY

This book is dedicated to all the exquisite women throughout my lifetime who have refused – whether consciously or otherwise, whether gently or with a fearsome ferocity to rival an awful August hurricane – to ever let me get away with living disconnected from my heart's deepest truth.

Contents

Praise for Tell the Truth, Let the Peace Fall Where it May

"Bryan Reeves takes the idea of telling "the truth, the whole truth, and nothing but the truth" to a deeper level. He's committed to an authentic search for the love that's at the heart of things, and reading his book you feel more committed to it too. He's a warrior for love in every sense of the word."
— *Marianne Williamson, #1* New York Times *Best-Selling Author*

"In a world plagued by ego-driven complexities, *Tell the Truth* has arisen to assist those craving a truly sacred existence. Bryan's work acts as a powerful mirror, allowing us to look within and without. He successfully uproots the seeds of untruths in our lives, holds our hands through the pangs of transformation, and celebrates the joys of living consciously. Our world needs more courageous voices like Bryan Reeves."
— *Lyric Benson Fergusson, Poet and #1 Amazon Best-Selling Author of* French Kissing God: A Journey to Enlightenment

"*Tell the Truth* reads like a nod to Ram Dass's classic, *Be*

Here Now. Bryan uses very personal stories, anecdotes, and most importantly, humor, as a means of sharing his journey towards living his truth and inspiring us to do the same...I loved it..."
— *Light Watkins, Creator of "The Shine"*

"I'm reading your book; I'm on the edge of my seat. I'm loving it; this totally flips me. It's fucking awesome. I love how you hold all the pieces, the light and the dark, so authentically. I so relate to everything you're saying and I am super excited for this to be in the world."
— *Ele Keats, Actress,* Newsies *and* Insidious 3

"If you're ready for revolutionary love, open these pages and let Bryan's crystal-clear insights magnetize you into action. This is the real deal!"
— *LeGrande Green, Host of "Be Bold" Podcast & Former* Oprah Show *Producer*

"Omg Bryan … My heart is overflowing reading your work … It's a 'master peace'!"
— *Robyn Chance, Artist*

Prologue

This book is the fruit of 20 plus years of my struggle to live with complete honesty about who I am. Every day.

I do not believe I am unique in western culture. I believe that our culture has such a deeply dysfunctional relationship with everyday truth and honesty that the vast majority of people experience lives they routinely feel disconnected from.

Tell The Truth, Let The Peace Fall Where It May is about coming clean down to the roots of your being. It's about walking through the world, through your entire life, in the fullness of who you really are.

You were born for greatness. But you can't build greatness on a foundation of bullshit.

This book is about three essential things:

(1) how and why most people live disconnected from their authentic truth everyday.

(2) what that chronic disconnection costs in joy, intimacy, fulfillment, vitality and more.

(3) what it could look like to live every moment in our authentic truth.

What makes living this way so insidious is we're often not even consciously aware we're doing it.

But your body always holds the truth.

When you act out of alignment with your deepest authentic truths in any moment, your body will usually inform you through anxiety, pain, discomfort, heaviness, illness, etc.

Perhaps you are believing a story about yourself, someone else, or about life that is not entirely true, and some deeper wisdom inside you instinctively knows it's not true. If you are acting from that false belief, particularly against your inner wisdom, then you are acting incongruently.

For the sake of this exploration, I will say you are lying to yourself – even if unconsciously so.

I certainly speak from personal experience, which you'll discover in this book.

If the word "lie" doesn't resonate with you because considering yourself a chronic liar is too big a stretch, then consider the word "incongruent." Might you be living incongruent with your deepest yearnings and soul desires?

We shall soon see.

We've been taught by our elders and the culture around us so many things about life, about ourselves and others that simply aren't true. We act out this programming even when we intuitively *know* it's not true. So powerful is our modern day worship of the intellect that we'll consistently let even our most shaky conclusions override clear evidence to the contrary.

This book will help you learn to distinguish between the lies your intellect tells you and the authentic truth your heart is always whispering through you.

You will explore where these lies come from and why you routinely choose to live inside them, disconnected from our authentic truths.

It may be that, as humans living in a dualistic world, there can be no direct experience of the truth without experiencing lies and disconnection, as well. In some ways, this has served powerfully to help us evolve and better know ourselves and our place in the universe.

Now, however, humanity's chronic disconnection, inauthenticity and incongruence has become too costly. Our planet is moving deeper into crisis on many fronts: environmental, economic, social, intrapersonal. We have made many improvements in our way of living throughout history, and everyday still brings exciting breakthroughs that offer hope for a more positive future.

But if we don't collectively get honest with ourselves and learn to live everyday in our most sincere personal truths, then even a technologically advanced future is destined to be a world full of conflicted people still longing for a home perpetually out of reach.

Ultimately, this book outlines what it can look like to live confidently in your full, authentic truth, throughout your life, everyday, trusting that the inevitable consequence of living in truth is that "peace" will effortlessly wrap itself all over you and wherever else it may … without you having to do anything else to make that happen.

A Note about Religious Truths and Absolute Truths

This book is not about absolute religious or philosophical truth. I'm not concerned about ancient stories of whose brother spited whom and whether we should pray five times each day or on Saturdays or only when bad things happen or at 4 PM every weekday on Channel 7.

I'm interested in the experience of speaking and living our own individual truths, the simple everyday truths we deny, ignore, doubt and distort to make ourselves more presentable, acceptable, powerful, lovable. These truths may embrace religious truths, but they are not limited by them. I want to both understand and bust out of those crazy self-imposed prisons we build on foundations of lies and misinformation. To be clear, that last sentence is not referring to religions as lies and misinformation, but rather the lies and misinformation we routinely stand on as solid reasons why we can't openly live our own unique truth, reasons we may not even be fully conscious of … and yes, reasons which may stem from religious beliefs that are in complete discord with our authentic truths.

A Book Is An Invitation Into Focused Contemplation

You may not accept all the ideas presented here, and I welcome your disagreement. I don't confess to have it all figured out. You'll quickly learn that I've made terrible mistakes that only the ignorant can make. I'm surely making the mistakes of the ignorant in my life today.

The invitation of this book is simply to dive deeper into your own self-discovery. Any worthy journey is not a matter of simply arriving at some destination. A worthy journey is one in which you are deeply transformed by the journey itself.

The treasures of the heart which we all seek are not available to those who simply hope to relocate from one unfulfilled spot to the next. This treasure only yields to those who conquer the inner dragons that guard it. For this shimmering mountain of heart treasure beneath the dragon's belly is none other than the pure, wild joy and passionate enthusiasm that can only be unleashed by living your authentic truth in every moment.

Let's begin.

We shall not cease from exploration, and the end of all our exploring will be to arrive where we started and know the place for the first time.
– T.S. Eliot

Part 1

The Roots & Rotten Fruits Of Deceit

1
The Messy Truth

For the first time I examined myself with a seriously practical purpose. And there I found what appalled me: a zoo of lusts, a bedlam of ambitions, a nursery of fears, a harem of fondled hatreds. My name was legion.
– C.S. Lewis

If I tell you the truth about who I really am, I'm afraid you won't love me.

For most of my life, I have lived with the constant fear that other people will reject me. I have lived so many years with the story that others are more deserving than I of all the good things in life: affection, attention, success, joy, satisfaction, happiness … love.

You wouldn't necessarily know it to be around me as I manage that fear well. It's a quiet fear that persistently suggests in the moments between more sane thoughts that other people are somehow better than I am; more whole, intelligent, happy, beautiful, generous, clear, righteous, courageous, strong, together, connected, aware. It insists I'm the only one who is clueless and confused in this world, and therefore I don't deserve love.

It's an insane fear, I know. Yet there it has persisted for years, lurking deep inside my thoughts like a poisonous thick mold in the dark vents of an otherwise lovely home.

Although this fear surely has its genesis in many experiences throughout my young life, one particular moment stands out when I began to suspect other people might be more worthy of love than I.

When I was three, my dad came to pick me up at Kinder-Care one day. I clearly remember him, bearded and boisterous, bounding into a playroom full of swarming toddlers like me. Just after he entered, I watched him bend over with a big jubilant smile on his face, arms wide open, and scoop a young boy up into those open arms with great cheer. That young boy wasn't me, and I didn't have a brother. I distinctly remember the shock of my three-year old brain seizing up, struggling to process this gross injustice it was witnessing, mortified at what it must mean.

To this day, I don't know if my dad did that as a joke, if he honestly mistook that other boy for me, or if I'm hallucinating the whole thing. Perhaps that little boy tripped on a skittle and fell into into the arms of my superhero dad who saved him from a bruised noggin.

Whatever actually happened, from the moment I saw that other kid get swept up into my dad's arms, I immediately began suspecting that other kids were more worthy of love than I. Over the years, I would add countless layers of evidence: dad leaving home for good when I was four; little girls running away from me on the playground; waking up alone in an empty home when I was five and not knowing that mom and sis had simply gone on a short walk; rejected by my best friend in 6th grade who chose the "cool" kids over me; and on and on and on.

Moments when I suddenly felt alone and unwanted were so deeply painful that I developed strategies to minimize the risk of them happening.

I wouldn't let girls I liked know that I liked them. I often shrank in social situations. I tried to share only the things about me that I hoped would make others like and admire me. I hid the thoughts, behaviors, ideas, curiosities and ignorances that I worried might offend or bore them.

Even as a young child, I experienced all kinds of wild commotion within me that the world around routinely insisted "good people" didn't experience: strong sexual attractions, anger, racist thoughts, dirty humor, mean, negative judgments and entirely selfish desires. Sure, lots of so-called goodness was happening within me, as well. But witnessing these "darker" experiences within, believing I couldn't safely share them with anyone lest I risk rejection, only deepened my worry that I wasn't worthy of love.

However, having now lived on this planet for 40-ish years through all variety of chaos, catastrophe and triumph alike, it is simply time to come out – and stay out – of the closet.

Embrace The Darkness Within

I have discovered I am everything.

I contain every possible aspect of the human experience.

Witty, insightful, arrogant, condescending, brave, mean, kind, loving, passionate, indifferent, courageous, smart, ignorant, cruel … I have been all of these in various moments throughout my life. So much so that I've come to realize these varying patterns of behavior are just little ever-changing wavelets atop a vast ocean of being that represents the full truth of *who I really am*.

By simply observing my inner world throughout my years, I have discovered, to both my joy and despair, that I can find within me every human emotion and behavior imaginable.

I am both heavenly lover and terrifying abuser. I have offered the highest praise to a beloved one day only to verbally torch some unsuspecting person on the next, even if only in my thoughts.

I am both wisdom and utter ignorance. I am steel-faced manly courage and yet also a scared, quivering little boy desperate for someone, anyone, to hold my hand and make the monsters go away.

I can be a brilliant, shining light radiating warmth and love in your presence. Yet when I'm cranky and un-mindful, I can also be a dark shadow waiting to storm havoc all over your lovely picnic.

I've experienced every genre of emotion and thought it seems a human being can experience. I am clearly everything. However, since nothing in that everything remains true all the time, I cannot be completely defined by any of it. Neither the admirable qualities nor the depraved ones can ever fully capture me.

I am somehow all of it, and yet none of it at the same time.

> *Do I contradict myself? Very well, then I contradict myself, I am large, I contain multitudes.*
> *– Walt Whitman*

Each of us contains within our own being the potential of the whole, both the good and the horrible.

A now famous Stanford University research study conducted in 1971 witnessed regular college student volunteers quickly begin psychologically torturing another group of student volunteers. The first group had been arbitrarily chosen to play "prison guard" and the other to play "prisoner." The researcher, who saw a dark nature of his own emerge during the experience, quickly shut down the study after just 6 days when the prison guard students turned dark, approaching sadistic, in a surprisingly short time. This experiment continues to shock us today as we are all still largely blind to the darkness lurking within each of us.

I experienced a similar descent into darkness in my own life many years ago when I got caught lying in the first few months of a new intimate relationship (I'll share more later). Although we stayed together, that partner vented her disappointment through intense anger. We were both deeply excited by and yet intensely terrified of each other.

I dealt with my confusion by trying to hide uncomfortable truths while she dealt with hers by turning emotionally, verbally, and even physically abusive. Before that relationship, I held righteous, indignant judgment towards any man who could be abusive in any way towards a woman, regardless the circumstances. Until my arrogant righteousness came crashing down when I followed her into that hell, and I too became abusive.

I would leave that relationship over and over, disgusted by who I was capable of being in her presence. After getting some distance and reconnecting with my more peaceful nature, I would go back to her. I desperately wanted that relationship to work. Each time, soon after I would return, my inner demons would reemerge and I would behave in ways I absolutely never believed possible. In retrospect, I now realize she was the perfect companion to help me explore the dark shadows in my own being I had never before dared enter.

Your vision will become clear only when you can look into your own heart. Who looks outside, dreams; who looks inside, awakes.
– Carl Jung

That relationship ended many years ago, and those fierce shadow demons I was dancing with seem largely exorcised. However, I can not forget my haunting experience in the darkness from whence they came, the darkness within me.

While I still strongly believe that no abuse, physical or emotional, is ever excusable, the capacity for even an avowed peace-maker to abuse shocked me awake to the dark, scary parts of myself I had never before explored. Before that relationship, like fleeing an unseen monster in a horrifying nighttime dream, I would flee into self-righteousness at the first hint of my own darkness, seeking false protection within whatever comforting light I could fabricate.

Of course, just as in our sleeping dreams, the inner monsters that we suppress inside and then project onto the outside world only continue stalking us. Until we confront them. For they are us.

In the case of that abusive relationship, I realize my ugly descent into such personal horror was entirely a result of my inability to tell the simple truth. I wasn't cheating on her or doing anything illegal. It was more subtle everyday things I wasn't being true about: *I'm confused. I'm hurt. I'm horny. I'm angry. I don't like how you talk about my friends. I don't like how you talk to me. I don't feel good giving you what you're asking for. I don't feel good in this conversation. I prefer to spend time alone right now. Etcetera.*

I could not consistently express the simple daily truths pulsing through my veins that constantly inspire me to action or quietly insist I take no action at all. Even in moments of clarity when I could, she could barely hear them. For she couldn't effectively express her truths, either. The persistent commotion of disconnection and incongruence in both our heads was far too loud for either of us to ever fully hear each other.

When we consistently deny these visceral everyday truths, they gather like insurgents who seek to paralyze us with fear, haunt our early morning dreams and torture us masterfully, without mercy, until our hearts are ripped bleeding fully open and we confess we were guilty all along.

The deep fear that I was unworthy of her love – unworthy even of love, itself – prevented me from openly confessing so many of these everyday truths. I would hide the truth about the turbulent rhythms of desire that changed in my body as our heart connection waxed and waned. I would disguise the profound ache that carved hollows in my chest whenever I felt attacked and invalidated. I would deny the confusion running rampant through my thoughts like an invasive weed. I would tell her I was all-in even as I silently prayed for escape.

I was so desperate for this beautiful woman to love and accept me, to validate me as a man, that I rarely allowed myself to be genuinely vulnerable in her presence. So I rarely told her the simple truths about me.

Truthfully, I was a mixed-nuts bag of confusion, fear, passion, love, innocence, arrogance, and everything in between. Rather than be openly honest about that, I instead conspired to twist "me" into something more stable that I hoped she would find palatable. Something safer. I didn't believe inside that I was worthy enough to have what I truly wanted. I pretended to be something she would approve of so I could have what she promised to offer: affection, sex, companionship, validation ... love.

Isn't it ironic that I sought validation of "me" by not fully being me?

I did not believe she would validate the authentic me. So I sought to win validation of a fantasy me that left out the inconvenient truths. I figured that would be enough to relieve my persistent angst.

Nope.

She would inevitably see through it, for I couldn't long maintain the ruse. But while I did maintain it, showing her the "me" I knew she wanted to see while hiding the "me" I knew she didn't, I was nonetheless aware of the deceit. Perhaps I hoped these uncomfortable inner truths would go away before she discovered them. They rarely did.

In the end, I spent four years in a relationship with a woman who could not accept me for who I am. Though to be fair, I didn't give her the chance, hiding "who I am" as much as I did.

It's water-drip torture to spend time with someone who doesn't accept you for who you are, who doesn't respect what's true for you.

The only reason you might ever choose to do that is that YOU don't accept you for who you are … *you don't accept your own authentic truth.*

What Silly Game Are You Playing?

We're all playing a game, and the game is to get whatever it is we think we want from the outside world; whether that be worldly success, wisdom, love, fulfillment, or simply the knowing that we have as equal a right to exist and be seen as anyone else.

Whatever game you're up to, you constantly engage strategies to get what you think you want. You may even be distorting your truth to make the outside world give you what you want, whether consciously or otherwise.

Pamela Myer, author of the bestselling book, *Liespotting*, says

Lying is an attempt to … connect our wishes and our fantasies about who we wish we were, how we wish we could be, with what we're really like. And boy are we willing to fill in those gaps in our lives with lies. On a given day, studies show that you may be lied to anywhere from 10 to 200 times. Now granted many of those are white lies. But in another study it showed that strangers lied three times within the first 10 minutes of meeting each other. We lie more to strangers than we lie to co-workers. Extroverts lie more than introverts. Men lie eight times more about themselves than they do other people. Women lie more to protect other people.

Clearly, we all wish things were at least a little different than they actually are. Many of us lie just to convince ourselves (and others) that they already are.

I've grown up with the persistent belief that if I were just different than I believe myself to be – if I were more successful, funnier, more charming or good looking – then I would finally be worthy of love.

In high school I was afraid to take off my shirt at the swimming pool because I didn't have a muscular physique. I was sure teenage girls would think lesser of me, because I thought less of myself. In my adult years, money became the thing I thought would get me love. A few times when my finances were precarious, I would pretend they weren't because I feared losing respect, and thus love – particularly from women, but from men, too. And so on.

Because I can never be different than who I am in any given moment, these mostly unconscious fears tempted me to create short-term experiences of skin-deep love rather than more rewarding long-term experiences of authentic love.

That's the secret game I've often played: I'll show you what I think you want to see, and you give me love.

Can you relate to that game?

Maybe your game is a bit different. Maybe you just want others to listen to or obey you. You might crave the experience of feeling significant. You might find yourself routinely covering up ignorance, fearful that if others discovered you don't really know what you're talking about, they won't respect you, listen to you or do what you say.

Perhaps your game is to get your needs met by someone else. That's an incredibly common game played by most of us, especially in intimate relationships. Maybe you use sex to get what feels like love. Maybe you use loving behavior to get sex. Or maybe you withhold one or the other as a power play substitute for confessing and working through your inner turmoil openly. People often fear that telling the raw truth risks losing the very thing they want most from their partners: full, loving presence.

And it might. Such may be the consequences of confessing the authentic truth.

Regardless, when you don't confess your real truths, you often later discover you've been playing the wrong game all along. You may get the trophy-respect you thought you needed, the trophy-partner you thought you wanted, someone may do what you want them to, and you might get all the money you thought would satisfy.

But whenever you sacrifice your authentic truth, you also sacrifice your authentic joy.

Live Your Truth or Sacrifice Your Joy

If you're not deeply satisfied with your life in every area, then you are likely in some meaningful way disconnected from your authentic truth. You may not be aware that you're playing the wrong game, but you're playing it. You're in a relationship, a profession or a job, a conversation, a mindset … you're willingly experiencing *something* that doesn't honor your authentic truth, because *you* don't honor your authentic truth.

If you're reading this book, you're probably aware on some level that you are not fully living in alignment with authentic truth(s) and are sincerely interested in stepping deeper into that experience. Regardless, if you're human, you're almost certainly experiencing some internal conflict between your authentic truth and your actual experience. It seems that basic conflict is coded into our DNA.

Because it seems we're each compelled to first explore the treacherous lands of *what and who we are* not as we journey towards the magnificent discovery of *what and who we truly are*. It's as if our authentic selves can only awaken like a mighty phoenix rising from the burnt black smoldering ashes of the false worlds precariously built by our disconnection and deceptions, which the truth eventually incinerates.

Even as I write this, there are areas in my life where I'm still not fully honest with myself or those around me. I've come a long way, but I'm writing this book in large part as self-administered therapy. The authentic truth sometimes still scares me silly.

We teach what we most need to learn.

The Truth in Your Thoughts

I have long asked myself, what really is the truth? What does it mean to live everyday in the authentic truth?

Years ago I read a book called Radical Honesty by Brad Blanton. That book, as I recall, advocated for admitting to the people around you every single thought that passed through your awareness.

If you don't like your boss, tell her so. Yes, you should tell your wife about your every lustful attraction to other women. If you can't stand the way your partner chews his food, you should say something about it. If you hate your mother-in-law's meatloaf, confess it right there at the dinner table. If you think your partner's ass looks big in those jeans, by all means tell her and be sure to do so with as much enthusiasm as you're actually feeling about it.

I tried radical honesty with a former girlfriend once. It was chaos.

I've read articles by journalists who took on the challenge, as well. Their experiences ranged from an ego-maniacal sort of liberated elation to "I'll never try that insanity again!"

Fortunately for spouses and mothers-in-law everywhere, I do not advocate for confessing every thought that occurs to you.

I'm actually distrustful of most thoughts. They have a life of their own, and they lie to us constantly. So many thoughts aren't even ours, but rather ideas we've accepted from the world around us. Many of our thoughts are also merely un-investigated judgments about other people, situations, cir-cumstances, events, ideas, etc. that don't reflect a deep authen-tic truth but a lazy opinion. Sometimes we would be well served by being quiet and listening more, inquiring more before we actually choose to express a thought in the world.

I am a passionate advocate for discernment. Which does not mean withholding the authentic truth. It means learning to separate our truth from our everyday insanity, which as you're about to discover, runs rampant in the human mind.

Life and Truth are Messy

The uncertain consequences of telling the full, simple truth frighten us. We really do believe – and in some cases may even be right – that if we confess our truths other people will aban-don or hurt us in some way. But when we manipulate from our disconnect with fantasies and lies, we're not giving anyone an opportunity to be with the real us, anyway.

I believe this is what most people truly want: *to be loved and seen for who we truly are, right now.*

When we tell the simple truth, as it arises in this moment, we give ourselves the chance to be loved for who we are. Those who can't be with us for whatever reason when we live openly from the authentic truths arising in our deepest heart, well, we're better off if they leave, anyway.

Whenever someone leaves me, I know I've been spared.
– Byron Katie

There's no guarantee that living from your deepest truth in this moment will get you what you think you want, at least not in external manifestations. Yes, your partner might leave you. You might lose a friend or a job. However, as my past relationship experience brought home to me, living with partners, friends, jobs, etc. that can't fully embrace who you are is an insidious and agonizing form of self-torture, anyway.

The simple truths are often uncomfortable only because our world runs so deep with beliefs that conflict with reality.

Life is messy. Being human is messy. It's not so neat as our "shoulds" and "shouldn'ts" would have us believe. We lust, we crave, we hurt, we fear; all of us experience all seven deadly sins.

Truth arises inside each of us in infinite ways. It takes shape as the good, the bad, the ugly and the beautiful.

Living your truth has little to do with anyone else. It's not merely about telling other people exactly what you're thinking right now.

No, it's far more exhilarating than that.

Confessing and living the truth of who you are in any moment ultimately yields only profound clarity, a deliciously deep abiding joy, and an effortless way of living that isn't possible when you're caught up living in the wild fictions of a conflicted, grasping mind.

But only when you don't expect the outside world to change as a result, or take any particular action at all. In allowing the outside world to not have to change as we confess our simple truths, to not have to fix what hurts or give us what we want, the only possible result is true freedom and genuine peace of mind.

Yes, it can take courage to accept whatever may be the consequences of living in your authentic truth. But only if you're attached to an outcome.

As we dive deeper in the following chapters, you're going to discover how living your authentic truth is its own succulent reward; and how forcing your jagged, chunky truth deep into your belly, hiding it from the rest of world, and especially from yourself, just cuts and bleeds you slowly from the inside.

You're going to learn it's far better to just spit it out, tell the truth and let the peace fall where it may.

REFLECTION QUESTIONS FOR JOURNALING

I encourage you to journal before continuing to the next chapter.

Reflecting gives you the opportunity to extract clarity and insight you may not yet be aware of. Writing is a tactile exercise that can help translate what your mind reveals into embodied, visceral wisdom.

Watch for shifts to happen (because "shift happens!") as your exploration continues.

Choose at least one question to explore:

1. Describe a painful event that happened early in your childhood when you created a story because of that event that has colored your entire life. Are you still living with that story?

2. Find examples in your life where you behaved in ways you never believed possible, even ways you would severely judge others for.

3. Find areas in your life where you are manipulating, deceiving, or hiding the truth from others (or yourself). What do you think you gain by doing so? What do you think you lose?

4. *What objections to this exploration are arising for you? Where do you believe living in your authentic truth would be inappropriate? Hurtful? Arrogant? Selfish?*

2

The Family: Training Grounds for the Art of Deceit

In a room where people unanimously maintain a conspiracy of silence, one word of truth sounds like a pistol shot.
– Czeslaw Milosz

We're natural born liars.

When we're very young, we literally die from lack of care and attention. So we instinctively use any method available to ensure we are seen and responded to! Even deceit.

As early as six months old, researchers have shown that we actually start to fake crying, injury, even laughter, to gain the attention of adults who can keep us alive.

Our lies get more sophisticated from there. By age two, we've perfected distraction and concealing forbidden behavior and are now moving on to the high-stakes art of bluffing.[1]

---

1. "Babies not as innocent as they pretend", The Telegraph, 7/1/2007, Richard Gray

Thing is, we never grow out of it, only better at it. And as we become adults we reinforce this behavior by encouraging our own young children to deny what they know to be true, too.

Anne Lamott, in her book *Bird by Bird*, writes about how intuitive thinking gets scraped out of us by our parents:

> *When we listened to our intuition when we were small and then told the grown-ups what we believed to be true, we were often either corrected, ridiculed, or punished. God forbid you should have your own opinions or perceptions – better to have head lice. If you asked innocently, 'Why is mom in the bathroom crying?,' you might be told, 'Mom isn't crying; she has allergies.' … And you nodded, even though you knew that these were lies, because it was important to stay on the adults' good side.*

Rather than effectively coaching our innate deceptive survival practices out of us (much like potty training coaches out our innate tendency to crap in our pants), our parents teach us almost as soon as we begin speaking that truth and intuitive knowing are dangerous subjects. We admire children's capacity to both pursue and then speak the truth while simultaneously doing our best to knock that instinct out of them.

Recall that classic scene in the movie *Uncle Buck* when John Candy gets grilled with rapid-fire direct questions by a focused, young McCauley Caulkin:

Miles (Caulkin): Where do you live?

Uncle Buck (Candy): In the city.

Miles: You have a house?

Buck: Apartment.

Miles: Own or rent?

Buck: Rent.

Miles: What do you do for a living?

Buck: Lots of things.

Miles: Where's your office?

Buck: I don't have one.

Miles: How come?

Buck: I don't need one.

Miles: Where's your wife?

Buck: I don't have one.

Miles: How come?

Buck: It's a long story.

Miles: You have kids?

Buck: No I don't.

Miles: How come?

Buck: It's an even longer story.

Miles: Are you my dad's brother?

Buck: What's your record for consecutive questions asked?

Miles: 38

Buck: I'm your dad's brother alright.

Miles: You have much more hair in your nose than my father.

Buck: How nice of you to notice.

Miles: I'm a kid – that's my job.

Curiosity is fundamental to our nature. We're fascinated by reality. Yet horrified by it, too.

With one breath we're instructed to always tell the truth, yet with the next we're told it's rude and shouldn't be spoken. We're scolded for lying about the cookie we lifted from the cookie jar, and then we're instructed to lie for daddy when he buys us ice cream and doesn't want mommy to know. Even when we tell the truth about taking the cookie (or just get caught with it in our little toddler mouths), we still often experience love being taken away by the very people we can least bear losing it from.

We learn very quickly that if we want to consistently maintain the experience of love, it's better not to always confess what's really up. Right out of the birth gate, our own instinctually deceptive strategies are reinforced by grown-up toddlers who never quite learned to fully face the more inconvenient realities of life.

It's no wonder we grow up completely perplexed by the truth and repeat the same patterns with our own children.

We Lie to "Protect" the Children

Like a lot of kids, I grew up unable to distinguish truth from lies in my home. I was four when my parents' marriage dissolved, along with any hope for verifiable truth. Each parent quickly became a political propaganda machine able only to spit out self-serving talking points.

I've never been able to separate fact from fiction about my parents' marriage, like what led to their divorce and the true nature of their youthful relationship. For a long time following their divorce, each parent seemed bent on casting reality in their own favorable light. I gave up asking years ago after both parents' lives had fully settled into new realities and the era of their marriage simply lost importance to me.

Variations of these scenarios play out in families all over the world.

Parents lie about their own youthful adventures, ostensibly to prevent their kids from doing the same things, and many even believe it works (my mom did; but it didn't). Adults lie about drugs, sex, death (*No honey, your hamster is only sleeping, though probably for a long time*). We shame kids out of touching themselves and getting to know their own bodies. We shield kids from nudity and words that aren't considered polite but that they obviously hear everyone use. We rip "imaginary" friends away from children, friends it seems they can literally see and touch, but then replace those imaginary friends with adult-approved fabrications like Santa Claus and the Tooth Fairy. Often, these sponsored lies become kids' first conscious exposure to the bewildering reality that adults actually lie – and with milk, cookies and money in hand!

Is it any surprise we find it so difficult to express our authentic truths as adults?

We're steeped in deceit from infancy.

One of the biggest lies in my family (that I'm aware of) was about drugs. When I was about 11, after we found the remains of a marijuana joint resting high on a kitchen shelf, my mom told me and my nine year old sister that she had never even been in the same room with someone smoking marijuana. She said she had no idea where that pungent little smoke came from. We were pre-teen, middle-class suburban kids, still watching cartoons and riding bikes after school. We had never seen drugs before. Had she told us it was just a rotten green bean we probably would have believed her. Who else would have brought it into the house but her or our step-father? Why was she so quick to deny?

Later, when I was a teenager, my best friend smoked marijuana in my home, marijuana we had found earlier that day in my step-father's dresser. I was too scared to touch it, but I wanted to witness what smoking it looked and smelled like, to stand by and marinate in the dangerous allure of this forbidden leafy fruit. My mom came home while we were in a basement bedroom, my friend smoking away using some tin-foil trick an older kid had taught him.

My mom pounded on the door, "Bryan! Is Tait in there smoking marijuana!?"

Jeeeeezzz! How in the world could she know Tait was in here smoking marijuana? How would she even know what it smelled like? … said her lie in my head.

I was horrified, petrified, panicked. Yes, of course, that we might be caught with marijuana, but even more so that she would find out it was her husband's pot. I surely would have told her, and then her lie would be exposed! The shame! The embarrassment! Truth suddenly popping out, like a rat running through a restaurant!

I dreaded the thought of all-powerful mom's lie unraveling, the Queen suddenly naked before her subjects. I feared revealing the lie more than I feared her growling fury on the other side of that way-too-thin, hollow bedroom door.

In a panic, I did the only thing I could think that might send her away. I told her she can't come in because Tait is naked. I offered no other explanation. "My best friend is naked in here and you can't come in," is basically what I said. I was 14.

During the tormented pause that followed, the entire house and surrounding woods held their breath. After eternity ended, I heard her feet shift as she turned and stormed up the stairs towards whence she had stealthily descended like a mom-ninja moments before.

Crisis over. Lies upheld. Truth averted. Delusional status-quo maintained.

She must have concluded in that exact moment that I was gay *and* a drug user. She's no homophobe, but it was probably too much to process right then. I don't know. We never spoke of it again. I think she figured out I wasn't gay when her Victoria Secret magazines began disappearing from the mail table and reappearing in discrete hiding spots around my bedroom. We never spoke about that either.

Not long after, in college, a roommate's giant marijuana bong triggered a flashback to an object from my childhood when I was only three or four years old.

This object is so prevalent in my early memories that it blends seamlessly into the fabric of my late 1970s youth, like my parents' scratchy zebra-striped couch.

It was like an older, wiser, stoic sibling who never spoke. It was about my height and slept in the kitchen pantry, just below the row of tall cereal boxes and our shiny silver waffle iron always caked with little creamy dabs and dribbles of puffy, dried batter.

My parents were always putting their mouths on this thing. I recall its tall, tubular smokey-orange see-through body with a short protruding handle near its bottom. Dark, milky constellations of soot ran the length of it like black lung disease.

This memory flash in the presence of my college friend's bong rang a bell so deafening that all the world fell silent as I suddenly discovered that I now lived in an entirely new universe – a universe in which my parents had a giant bong when I was three.

I now had overwhelming evidence that my mom was just completely full of adult duplicitous bullshit, and I was furious. I never spoke to her about it, still afraid to confront this reality she seemed so resistant to dealing with, and it took me years to forgive her without her ever knowing why I was angry.

I have a great relationship today with my mom. I have for most of my life. She's actually one of the most extraordinary people I know, and easily one of the most honest and trust-worthy. Yet she still felt compelled to lie to her children in an effort to protect us from … something. It's hard to really grasp the direct results. It certainly did create a time where I resented her. My sister was a much more adventurous teenager than I. She did what she was probably going to do anyway, regardless of whether mom ever copped to having a bong or not. She smoked pot as a teenager. As for me, when I left the military at age 26 and finally felt free of all the heavy moral and legal constraints I had been wearing for so long, I sought out marijuana like a pot-seeking missile.

The First Moment of Truth

Most kids experience some variety of youthful rebellion, which typically involves lying and saying pretty mean things to our parents. However, when we begin speaking from our deepest truths and we know doing so is likely to painfully con-front our parents, that is when we truly begin our transition into adulthood.

I remember the first time I consciously spoke from my own genuine truth in a way that challenged my father. I was around 19, and I don't recall ever being invited to counter my father's ideas up to that moment. He wasn't tyrannical by any means. He just spoke so self-assured that there wasn't invitation for debate. I also didn't grow up living with him, since he and my mother separated when I was four. Thus he loomed large and infallible in my imagination, his real humanity filtered out by the geographic distance between us. He was a superhero in my mind. How could a young boy possibly challenge a superhero?

Even in that moment, when I was 19, I wasn't invited to challenge him. But I finally hit my tipping point as shaky words fumbled from my mouth in bold protest of what seemed absurd words coming from his.

My father, a legitimately brilliant man, was fascinated at that time with global conspiracy theories, secret alien technologies, psychic phenomenon and that sort of thing.

I'd been hearing his fascinating perspectives much of my life, and I mostly enjoyed them as they added a wild, exciting dimension to life. But I was a young man now in college exploring my own independent mind. This was the first time I had ever dared propose that he might be wrong.

What if he suddenly decided to pick up and love that other little kid again? I was literally trembling.

I didn't know what would happen. I didn't fear he would physically hurt me. I feared more that, as with my mother's absurd lie about marijuana, I would somehow diminish his stature on the planet. I didn't want to be the son tossing his weakened father victoriously from his throne of omnipotence. I feared he would not survive the fall!

For months I had been been privately doubting his sometimes wildly conspiratorial insights. It seemed he was handing them off to me like small firearms I was supposed to use when sinister Big Brother finally kicked in our door.

In all fairness to him, he's mostly crazy in the good kinds of ways. He is remarkably insightful, able to see past the veils most people can't see past, or refuse to. With great gratitude I credit him (and his wife, my step-mother) for teaching me to investigate beyond the obvious and take nothing at face value, especially if it comes from politicians, journalists, history books, or alien lizard people (I've yet to meet one of those, as far as I know).

But all these conspiratorial stories simply started to overwhelm me. It's like saying the word "spaghetti" over and over again; the word loses all meaning and you get discombobulated. You lose the ability to function in normal spaghetti-eating society. The word just disintegrates into useless nonsense when all it's trying to do is name a long, skinny piece of carbohydrate. I'm just saying I enjoy my conspiracy theories in small doses, like an annual shot of tequila. I'm no good to anyone if I'm drunk every day, or if I'm muttering over and over the word "spaghetti."

So I stood up to my dad, nauseous and quivering – that's why I still remember it to this day. In my memory, it took him by surprise. He'd never been questioned by his son like this before. We had never actually shared an adult-like conversation with opposing conclusions until that moment. I had been too afraid to challenge him and risk losing his love again.

My thoughts had me convinced for years that might be the consequence of challenging him. After all, it seemed to have happened before when I was just standing there doing nothing but inhabiting my body. If I actually took him on and challenged him, surely he would withdraw his love from me. So I thought.

Fortunately, in this initial challenge when I was 19, he seemed to survive the fall. He probably wouldn't even agree that he fell. It wasn't about him, anyway. It was about me, finally standing for my own truth. After a few minutes of intellectual parrying – him maneuvering to ground his story in reality, me retorting with scientific principles and the logical arguments of simplicity – the conversation turned abruptly, awkwardly, to dinner.

Whereas moments before I had been but a timid boy, I now experienced the invigorating, powerful internal sparks of manhood-onset.

Yes, I know that may sound ridiculous. Our culture does not practice many rites of passage for boys to become men. We have no death-tempting vision quest; we are not sent into the wilderness naked and thirsty to face wild demons. Getting a driver's license, drinking a beer at 21, touching a classmate's private bits, all landmark moments. But few moments can compare to the first time we challenge the authority of our parents from the deep grounding of our fragile inner truth.

My experience may be lame compared to other people's first grown-up moments of daring contradiction. But it was a momentous day for me. It was the first time I risked the consequences of speaking an opposing truth, my truth, to my larger-than-life father.

Even today I sometimes feel intimidated standing up to my dad. That is probably why I often do it with more *enthusiasm* than necessary. I still sometimes need a running start.

But that's how I learned to speak truth to my father: by simply speaking it.

It's Necessary to Rebel Against Your Parents' Agenda

Many of us harbor mommy and daddy issues so deep that the thought of disappointing them seems worse than simply living a lie. A consequence of our society's dysfunction around the truth, living out our parent's agendas instead of our own is one of the most disconnecting, deadening choices we can make. People routinely live such incongruent lives for decades, suffering a quiet, unhurried demise, hopelessly estranged from their heart's deepest yearnings.

My struggle with living truth in the face of my father took on a new urgency when he began rejecting the girlfriends I would bring to family dinners.

I was mortified that he would brazenly question my most personal of choices. A battle within me began to rage. Sometime that rage exploded towards him and my anger would rattle the walls. Other times I kept quiet, simmering hot like a volcano on the verge.

Though I refused to admit it, I didn't realize I was only mortified he might be right, that I was choosing my partners primarily out of insecurity and fear. I was not aware that my battles with him were really only the projected version of the battle I was fighting within myself.

This happened to two of the most important female relationships in my life.

My father would ignore them at family gatherings, denounce their motives – which he could only guess at, for he never really took any time to know them – or question their suitability to my face. I would never become the man he wanted me to become if I chose that woman, he would not-so-subtly imply. He never included them in invitations and was awkward and cold when I brought them to dinner.

I so desperately wanted my choices to meet his approval. But my stubborn pride also didn't want to prove him right, thus proving me wrong.

My pride and his rejections made things harder when I was considering whether to end my relationships. I was determined to be sure I decided things on my terms, because a relationship genuinely wasn't right for me, not because of his unwanted opinions.

Ironically, my stubborn refusal to allow his influence probably kept me in these relationships longer than I should have stayed. Resentment towards him swelled in me like a hot air balloon filled with bile, and that anger obscured my self-awareness.

His behavior incensed me and broke their hearts. I remember

one of those girlfriends crying sweetly on the way out of his home one evening. She tried her best to wear a brave face, but she was crushed that the father of the man she loved refused to even acknowledge her presence.

The only woman he ever quickly accepted into his world was a domineering French woman I then quickly married. On some level, his approval brought relief and strengthened my intention to hold on to this one. Deep inside, I still wanted to please Daddy – I wanted his love. I wanted him to pick me up at Kinder-Care; not some other kid! For that, I was willing to deny my own intuitive knowing that this marriage was going to be a disaster.

Which it was. I remember the day before our wedding, a little voice whispered to me incessantly, calmly: *This is going to destroy you.*

Indeed, within a very long eight months it did destroy me (which ultimately served me well, though that exploration is for another time). That relationship was ironically one of the least satisfying in my life, even before we married. It's not coincidental that it was also the only girlfriend of mine my father ever accepted and approved of. I was the one who walked down the aisle, but clearly my father had no better insight into what was good for me than I did.

Sometimes the deepest truth a parent can connect with completely opposes your own.

Obviously, if you discover over time that you can't bring a sensible partner home that your parents approve of, it's tempting to stop bringing them home or even coming home altogether. Likewise if our parents reject any of the choices we've made, we may grow weary of defending ourselves and trying to change their antiquated brains.

Anyone who's ever had a parent, a child or a sibling – which should cover just about everyone – has experienced the scratchy discomfort of an ill-fitting family agenda. For most, the experience lies closer to the resentment held against your parents for not liking your new boyfriend. For an unfortunate few, however, it occurs more like horror when dad points a shotgun at your head as you're about to confess your homosexuality, which happened to a close friend.

Except in the most open-minded families, it can take tremendous courage to consistently live your authentic truth openly before family. From simply suggesting a parent's conclusion is wrong to living a sexuality that horrifies them, it takes courage.

Family – particularly parents, but siblings, too – think they know you. They think they've got you figured out. They have good reason to think so, having birthed and raised you and all. It's still not true.

When you stray beyond the boundaries and expectations that family has created in their own minds for you, it can be confusing for them, even threatening. Depending on their own level of self-awareness, they may go so far as resent your successes, chide you for your apparent failures, cast doubt on every choice you make, even get angry with you for divorcing that nice young, wealthy man. There's no end to the harsh judgments our families can throw at us, all based on stories they believe about who we are and what we should be doing.

As you grow and evolve, exploring beyond the boundaries they've set for you – and that you've set for yourself – new aspects of you surface that perhaps no one ever witnessed before, not even you. Sometimes you come by these new aspects of being by making mistakes. Mistakes that maybe your parents or peers see coming, but that you've got to experience for yourself.

Newer Generations are Evolution In Action

My mother, bless her generous, kind heart, has been a huge supporter of most of my choices in life. However, she's always worried for me around money. I've been a wild adventurer, reckless even. I've backpacked Third World countries alone, run away with a music band, married a mysterious French woman, and repeatedly left great-paying, secure jobs to follow the call of adventure. Money has been a roller-coaster experience for me, and my mom knows it.

I know my explorations make her a bit uncomfortable. She supports me, and she knows I always find a safe place to sleep, but she worries for me. Her life has been characterized by steady, meaningful work. Until the last 10–15 years, most generations came of age in the era when people worked for one or two companies their entire adult lives. It's a new concept for my mom's generation that people would explore new work, even completely change professions, every 3–5 years.

Then there's me, an ambitious and intelligent man, former Air Force officer capable of working for any great company, who's also an irrepressible adventurer, a life long philosophical seeker, an entrepreneur, and an artist. The thought of working for one company my entire life is madness. I'm beyond my mom's comfort zone.

This is how evolution works. With new energy and fresh eyes, the young explore the world around them as it exists today. We tease and test and push beyond the boundaries that our ancestors, even the living ones, created. In the unknown, unexplored realms, we young at heart both triumph and make awful mistakes, which we hopefully learn from.

In this way we courageously map the unknown realms so the generations to come need not repeat our adventures, but can make their own by venturing even further out, mapping the unknown we could not get to. By leaping from the broad shoulders of the pioneering generations before us, the known universe expands.

The duty of youth is to challenge corruption.
– Kurt Cobain

It's the birthright of the younger generations and the young-at-heart to push past the boundaries fought for and staked by previous generations who can no longer explore or have simply tired of the exercise. Many of our parents have stopped exploring, stopped pushing beyond any boundaries and may have accepted their own as absolute for all.

As we blow right past their ill-fitting boundaries and come to know ourselves in light of a larger world, our new ways of being may frighten and intimidate those who stayed behind. We're certainly bound to confuse all but the most open-minded of our elders.

Family Misery Demands Company

The Indian teacher, Osho, said:

> People are afraid of those who know themselves. They have a certain power, a certain aura and a certain magnetism. ... The enlightened man cannot be enslaved – that is the difficulty – and he cannot be imprisoned. Every genius who has known something of the inner ... is going to be an upsetting force. The masses don't want to be disturbed, even though they may be in misery they are accustomed to the misery.

Osho also said, "to those living in misery, anybody who is not also living in misery looks like a stranger."

Misery indeed loves company.

As we live further into our authentic truth, we experience more and more the juicy magnificence of knowing ourselves. We watch the lies that envelope us, the imaginary boundaries originally fashioned by other people dissolve back into the shadowy realm of limited-mind from whence they came.

Watching these lies dissolve away like funky mold in bright sunshine, we learn to live more and more on the thrilling edge of possibility. Every new moment shows up bursting with potential adventure.

As we come to truly know ourselves and live out our unique expression of life, if the people in our families are not similarly ripening, expanding their boundaries and still seeking to broaden their own perspectives, then our freedom, our joy, our truth may actually offend them.

After all, it's much easier for people living stagnant lives to look outward and make judgments about other people's lives, rather than acknowledge the lethargic, possibly decaying state of their own and make new, uncertain choices.

Anyone who might negatively judge us or even attempt to proactively disadvantage us, whether family or not, could only do so under the spell of their own inner turmoil.

Genuinely satisfied, happy people waste little time offering unsolicited criticism about others' choices. They're too busy enjoying their own lives to bother. If you are deeply connected and contented with your choices, deeply contented people connected to their own truth will respect, even celebrate you.

Nonetheless, when our families condemn us, the discomfort we feel can lead us to put the relationship on ice ... or to just lie.

In either case, we lose what could be a precious relationship with our immediate family. Granted, in some cases the family vitriol may be so corrosive that it's legitimately better to sever the relationship and withdraw.

In many cases, though, I believe our families mean well and just want to see us happy and successful, but are simply bumping into the limitations of their own beliefs about the world, and thus themselves and you, too.

Unity Reverend James Trapp once said, "Our parents birth us physically, but we birth our parents spiritually."

Could it be that being your authentic true self, even if they don't understand or support it, is the greatest gift you could actually give your parents?

Denying The Truth = Suffering

In the end, denying your authentic truth for fear it will be used against you is an ultimately exhausting attempt to manipulate your family (or anyone) into believing you are something you are not. Either that, or it's a futile attempt to actually make yourself into something you think they'll approve of, but also that you are simply not.

Truth is, if they're inclined to disapprove of your authentic self – or the partner you bring home – they'll still find things about you to disapprove of even while you're pretending to be what they want.

The consequence is inevitably suffering. Certainly yours. Theirs, too, from either suffering the pain of shock and disillusionment when the truth finally does come out, or missing out on the unique, never-before-seen brilliance you alone came here to express.

Of course, even if your family can't appreciate your unique brilliance, in a world of 7 billion people, there are countless others who can. Why deprive them, too?

Fortunately, negative judgments and bad behavior by our family and friends can push us even deeper into exploring who we really are. We get to experience the harshness of their thoughts infesting our own. As these negative ideas churn like bitter buttermilk in our thinking, over time life gives us plenty of opportunity to discover whether they really ring true.

If we can breathe through the anxiety of not having our loved ones' approval and not resist the distasteful perspectives they introduce, we can discover even more who we are by discovering through those crazy ideas clearly who we are NOT.

Inauthenticity, lying and deceit, unfair judgments, all are an inherent part of our childhood family experiences. This is life's first great obstacle course training us in the art of discernment around what is truth and what is pure fantasy.

Granted, it can be a brutal obstacle course that also leaves us wounded, bleeding, and with a few wicked scars.

As we mature into adulthood and finally leave our parents, we soon take whatever wisdom we learned – and whatever coping mechanisms we created to survive – into our own intimate relationships.

Thus begins a whole new adventure in the wilds of authenticity.

REFLECTION QUESTIONS FOR JOURNALING

Choose at least one question to explore:

1. What were the predominant lies and disconnects you grew up with in your family? Were there uncomfortable aspects of your family that would have been healthy to openly address but weren't? If so, what stories and beliefs supported silence around those issues?

2. Can you find anywhere in your life where you might be living to your parents' agenda, whether to prove them right about you, or perhaps prove them wrong?

3. What kind of climate do you aspire to create in your current family? Is openness and honesty genuinely welcomed? If someone in your family shares an uncomfortable truth, are they received with understanding and kindness? Or are they shamed and "taught a lesson"?

4. If you have kids, are you lying to them about something or pretending something is different than it really is? If so, why? What do you hope to accomplish? How successful do you think you'll be?

3

Truth and Intimate Relationships

You'll hate me for the truth before you love me for a lie ...
and I wouldn't want it any other way.
– Evette Carter

My mom once said it's plain stupid for couples to always tell the truth to each other. I was a bit young at the time, so I didn't get whether she meant that it's merely pointless to tell each other absolutely everything or that strategic proactive lying is advisable if you want to survive a lifetime with another human being.

Whatever she meant, some form of lying is the reality for most couples. Whether pretending everything's ok when you're actually fuming, faking an orgasm, or outright infidelity, lying in intimate relationships is common as a sigh. Most of us grow up in families that don't cultivate a consistent healthy relationship to authentic being; why should we expect much different in our adult intimate relationships?

Intimate relationships are where the truth often scares us most because it's where the stakes seem highest. In the mysterious world of intimate relationship with another, we believe we stand to gain – or lose – everything.

That belief is evolving as our culture evolves and we are more eager than ever to experience other aspects of life independent of intimate relationships, such as travel, adventure, career.

Nonetheless, intimate relationships remain that wondrous arena in which we may transcend our limitations to taste the most ecstatic of human experiences, and in which we may also die a million tiny deaths as life cuts and bleeds us over and over and over.

The Myth of "You Complete Me!"

Love finds us everywhere. You could be on a short anthropological African safari to study the mating habits of wildebeests, and one day the pilot bringing monthly food rations lands with his cute son in tow. He splits his saltine cracker and hands it to you with a gentle smile, the butterflies gather and that's it. You're over the moon and moving to Zaire.

Most of us think what's happening is we're finally getting what we always wanted. Yippee! Sex, love, companionship, family, more money, security, protection, an extra helping of saltine crackers, etc. We may get all or most of those things, if we're lucky. We often learn too soon, however, we're not getting the easy-bake deal we thought was ours.

Unfortunately, from the young age we start watching fairy tale movies, our entire cultural paradigm conditions us to think a partner will complete us, as if we were a broken, sad-faced coffee mug in search of our missing magic handle. If you complete me, you obviously have the power to render me once again incomplete. If I tell you a truth you don't like, you could leave me, abandon me, dislike me, degrade me, deny me, punish me; you could turn me back into a pathetic lonely coffee mug with no magic handle.

In other words, you could destroy me. So I better be cautious with "the truth."

Among the most fateful decisions I ever made was one simple, seemingly inconsequential lie I chose to tell a woman I would have likely married otherwise, if not for that lie.

It happened in the first two weeks of our new romance when she was openly commitment-averse. She insisted she didn't want to be in a relationship with anyone.

Since we weren't in a "relationship" I decided it wasn't her business what I had just done on *my business* trip to Switzerland. I chose not to confess that I took a short romantic trip to France with an Indonesian woman I had been seeing in the midst of my jet-setter lifestyle at that time.

So far, so fine. No lie; just my own personal business I was not bound by any agreement with her to share.

However, within hours of arriving home, Valerie (not her real name) asked me with probing, hesitant eyes, "Were you a good boy on your trip?"

Rather than honor the truth of my choices and invite a vulnerable, real discussion into the nature of our budding relationship, I assured her with a nervous smile that, "Yes, I was a good boy on my trip."

I had decided I would not see the other woman again, anyway, so I took the easy road – or so I thought. I lied.

That lie changed the course of my life. In some ways, it was the genesis for this book, although I had no idea at the time. Had I known what consequent horrors I was setting both Valerie and myself up for, I would have never … *never* … told the lie. But this was a lesson I apparently wanted to learn the exceedingly painful way. Valerie also clearly wanted to learn some things.

She discovered the lie four months after I told it, on the exact day we were planning to officially commit to a monogamous relationship.

She found date-stamped pictures on my computer of that side-trip excursion with a beautiful Indonesian woman at my side. I don't know whether this spooky coincidence reaffirms my belief that there are no mistakes in the universe, or whether it underscores the impossible randomness that governs our lives. It certainly suggests a universe that enjoys justice and excruciating irony.

I was at the grocery store, standing in the chilled dairy section, picking out whipping cream for a delicious strawberry dessert

I would prepare for our commitment ceremony that evening, when my cell phone rang.

I answered excited and happy. I could hear immediately something was wrong. Her voice was seething with icy rage.

She asked about my trip to France ... *No*. She didn't *ask*. She *insisted*. She already knew. Standing there in that stark, fluorescent-lit grocery isle, the axis of my world tilted catastrophic and my body filled with sickening nausea.

I dropped the hand-basket where I stood and flew home to avert disaster. Before I could even talk, she furiously demanded that I delete every aspect of our four months together from my life; that I remove her pictures from my computer, her number from my phone, her memory from my brain synapses.

I was devastated. Just an hour prior I had been smiling, warm and content before the glorious gates of paradise. Now, I was paralyzed in mid-air as life surprise-drop-kicked me towards a land of hell and fury.

Valerie's crazed reaction at merely discovering the pictures so terrified me that I couldn't imagine what she might do if she knew the full truth, that I hadn't been a "good boy" in Europe. But she still had no real evidence of that. Yes, she had seen pictures of me in France with another woman, but I quickly decided I could still pull this off.

I so feared her leaving me that I confessed to the France trip but insisted like a guilty president before the world that I did not have sex with that woman!

I hadn't been this deeply excited about a woman in years. What if Valerie was the woman I was meant to marry? What if she was my missing magic handle?

I couldn't bear losing her now.

So I lied. She hardly believed me. I dug in.

During the four-year relationship with Valerie that miraculously followed, our interaction deteriorated into an angry, hopeless place devoid of trust and all respect. That first lie was the "original sin" of our relationship. It's not that simple, of course. But that initial lie – and my inability to immediately, fully account for it and apologize – helped set our tortuous fate in motion.

Rather than move maturely together through this awkward revealing of truth, we stayed together but dug into our positions. She began telling herself and me the story that I was a disgusting, horrible, worthless liar. I began telling us both that she was a spiteful, abusive, overreacting child.

Thus we regressed into screaming toddlers battling endlessly over who hit who first. We stayed together, fighting this impossible war, for four desperate ... chaotic ... heart-wrenching years.

I finally surrendered the full truth of my trip to France six months after she found out. By this time, I was completely worn down by the emotional abuse. Sadly, any remaining safe haven for honesty and love between us had been infiltrated by our hateful war parties, lined with radioactive explosives and obliterated. Our nightmare was still only beginning.

Relationships Surface Unhealed Wounds

In intimate relationships, unhealed wounds can rise violently to the surface when triggered.

A few years before she met me, Valerie had run away from a marriage after discovering her husband was lying about his infidelity with another woman. He never confessed the full truth, and she never dealt with the anguish of that experience. She just up and ran away from the man she had loved since she was 14.

Then I came along, a man she would fall for quickly, and I ambushed her with a lie that rang despairingly familiar.

But I lied early in our relationship, before we even agreed to having one. I believe that fact made the offense ambiguous enough for her to stay, yet still betrayal enough for her to rage – and rage she did against the perceived injustice that both her ex-husband and I had perpetrated against her, as well as anyone else who ever lied to her in the past leaving her feeling vulnerable and powerless. I received the full assault. Her ex-husband was mostly spared.

Of course, my lie was itself merely the iceberg tip of an unhealed wound surfacing quickly in the relationship: my belief that I wasn't worthy of love. If I told her who I really was, and what I was really capable of, she wouldn't love me. Thus our relationship began to descend into dark shadows.

Many people spend a slow lifetime unearthing and working through the unseen shadow aspects of their being, if they ever do so at all. We got to it quickly!

The renowned psychiatrist Carl Jung is famous for elucidating the importance of exploring and bringing the so-called shadow into conscious awareness. He believed this was essential for the person to incorporate the best of what is unseen within us, and also to end the reign of terror perpetrated by the worst of it.

Though we certainly shared wondrous beauty and sweetness at times, the darkness that seethed throughout much of our four-year relationship was an obvious consequence of not telling the truth. I don't mean just that first lie. I mean every lie, from her ex-husband's lie to my original sin, to the lies Valerie's hateful judgments told about me for years, as well as the ones my judgments told about her. Our lives were flooded with a brackish mix of blame and contempt and paranoid delusions, half-truths, complete truths, honest denials and plenty of dishonest ones, too.

Our intense attraction insisted the other was the missing puzzle piece that would restore wholeness. We worked desperately to fix our problems, which in our ignorance translated to insisting the other person change to meet our satisfaction.

After all, "if you're my missing piece, you better damn well get with my program and act like it!"

As our wounds awakened and roiled in raged, we burned in a hell of our own imagining.

Relationships Are Doorways To Your Self

Clarissa Pinkola Estes writes in Women Who Run With The Wolves, a masterpiece tome about the ancient mythological stories of the Wild Woman archetype:

> *He does not realize that he is bringing up the scariest treasure he will ever know, that he is bringing up more than he can yet handle. He does not know that he will have to come to terms with it, that he is about to have all his powers tested. And worse, he does not know that he does not know. That is the state of all lovers at the beginning: they are blind as bats.*

Blind as bats we are upon entering the intimate dance with another.

We think this other has come to complete us, save us, rescue us from our emptiness, loneliness and despair. And it may appear they do save us, for a time. Until we realize we've hooked "the scariest treasure" we will ever know.

When we discover that our partners don't complete us, nor

could they – usually after endless disappointments and disillusionment have led us to abandon all hope of "being completed" by another – that's when our real work begins.

For this is when we begin to truly meet ourselves.

When I got married at 26 in France, I was so wounded from the military and father stuff that all I wanted was someone to give me the love I couldn't find within myself.

I married thinking I had finally found a true source of love: Her.

Well, she quickly blew up that delusion!

During our brief eight-month marriage I made her completely responsible for my happiness and well-being. Which is a delicious recipe for disaster in any relationship, but especially in ours, for *we did not get each other at all*!

She never appreciated my jokes, nor I her's. I wanted a good-morning kiss everyday; she just wanted to be left alone. She smoked constantly; I loathed cigarettes. She walked faster than I did so she was always 20 feet ahead of me on the street; you wouldn't even know we were together. I wanted a lot of sex; she mostly wanted a lot of sleep, going so far once as to blame her disinterest on the weather. She wasn't giving me love in any way I could recognize!

I should mention that we married five weeks after we met. The idea arose as mainly a legal immigration exercise so I could get papers to stay and work in France. But we were dating and already sleeping together, and I now saw her as my source of love. It became a real marriage, real fast.

I was a young man, fresh out of the military, disconnected from the wisdom of my heart. She was a strong independent woman with a diagnosis of bi-polar disorder. We would turn out to be great teachers for each other!

For this ill-conceived marriage was a rude awakening for me … to myself. During these eight months, my eyes began opening to just how self-centered, narcissistic and incapable I was of giving authentic love to an intimate partner.

The moment I first glimpsed this was both shocking and heartbreaking.

It happened one chilly sunset evening on a wind-swept mesa in Mallorca, Spain, where I took us for a December honeymoon with a $1000 wedding gift from my uncle. We had already been married for four months, yet the catastrophe was well underway.

We hadn't had sex in the last three months of our four month marriage. I was an increasingly disgruntled stay-at-home dad to a cute patch-eyed French Bulldog and her big Boxer sister. She was doing her medical internship 70 hours a week, so I rarely saw her, and when I did, she never gave me what I wanted.

The first night of our honeymoon, after she went once again to sleep without wanting sex, I went for a walk and slept in the rental car. It was our honeymoon! Why wasn't she giving me the love I wanted?

I spent the next three days steaming, sulking, doing my bare-minimum best to show her a good time while withholding as much enthusiasm, appreciation and contentment as I could to punish her with their absence.

Thus went our honeymoon: awkward and uncomfortable.

Until the fourth day, her birthday. I intentionally gave her no special treatment that day. She noticed.

Later that evening, as we drove up a steep winding road towards an old monastery resting majestic atop one of Mallorca's ancient mesas, we began to argue about love. I assured her I knew what love was and how to do it, and if she would just listen and act the way I described, our relationship could be amazing. She objected, offering her own evidence that I was in fact the one who did not know how to love, including today, her birthday, and how I gave her no special birthday treatment.

I parked the car in the gravel lot at the entrance to the monastery. She got out and started walking off in that fast paced way she had about her. I scrambled after her, throwing condescension and arrogance at her back as I struggled to keep up. She hustled across the monastery courtyard towards the edge of the mesa where the sky was in full sunset regalia, exploding into wispy streaks of orange and red and violet. The ancient monastery was quiet, deserted, somber as a graveyard.

I chased her all over that ancient mesa, spouting the trite wisdom of a 26-yr old clueless man as the sky turned to dark ominous shades of navy and purple.

It was an epic scene.

When we finally got back into the car, I could sense that she had given up.

I knew then if we left this mesa without some breakthrough, our marriage was over. I wasn't ready for that. So I sat there, my hands on the wheel, key in the ignition, going nowhere.

I stopped speaking. I saw she had no more fight left in her.

With a deep sigh of utter resignation, she asked me to start the car and just get going. She didn't even care where. But I sat there. Waiting. For what, I did not know.

She let out another sigh and stared silently out the window into the dark.

Everything went quiet in that car on an ancient mesa in Mallorca, two humans sitting hushed and still beside one another, desperate for love but lost and unsure from where to summon it.

Quiet as a monastery.

I suddenly saw from outside myself this young ignorant boy sitting next to his newly-estranged wife in a rental car on a cold December night, not just refusing to drive away but actually unable to. As I considered the situation, I turned my head away from her resignation and looked down at the key ignition that I could not turn to ignite.

Something within me breathed a deep breath, and I surrendered.

Which is when it rushed through me.

A profound clarity then flashed into my awareness like light from a cresting sunrise. Just then I knew why I had married this woman: *She was to teach me how to love even when I wasn't getting anything in return for it.*

My mothers and sisters had always doted on me growing up, the only son, the only brother. It was easy to love them well. Every past girlfriend had always given me more or less everything I wanted, from affection and sex to respect and admiration. It was easy to believe I loved them well, too.

I had been totally unaware about how poorly I loved when I did not get what I wanted.

This infuriating woman, the first who would give me none of what I really wanted from a woman, I married her. I had to. She was the first of my lessons in learning to *love anyway.*

She was the doorway to discovering my truest self, the love that I already am.

Blind as a bat I had been ... until that moment on the mesa.

This of course was only the start of a long transformational journey that continues to this day. The French woman was my entrance exam to the PhD program of Valerie.

For she kicked me out of our home a few months after Mallorca, despite my fiddling new efforts to offer love no matter what she gave me in return.

But now I was attuned to new possibilities for *living as love*, rather than merely living just to get it.

Sadly, many people live entire lives completely focused on what they're getting from an intimate relationship: "If he/she would only … [fill in the blank] … get their shit together, be more thoughtful, touch me more, say nicer things, listen for once, stop being selfish, honor their word, spend more quality time, give me more space, etc. … then I can be genuinely happy."

In that thinking, upset will always be my reaction when my partner doesn't give me the attention, affection, validation, respect, love I want, the way I want it, whenever I want it and as long as I want it for.

By focusing on what my partner can be doing to make my life better, I fail to grasp that this untamable, perplexing, and sometimes maddening woman before me is actually a pathway to the most profound adventure of discovering my own elusive true self.

"It is your soul's work to not overlook what has been brought up [when you begin a new love], to recognize treasure as treasure no matter how unusual its form, and to consider carefully what to do next," says Clarissa Pinkola Estes.

I can hardly say I chose carefully, in my complete ignorance of what was happening. I simply stayed – with my wife for eight months until she kicked me out; with Valerie for four years, despite the nightmare I was living.

What was really going on? Why was I choosing these painful experiences?

Because I had brought up "the scariest treasures," and my soul was yearning to learn how to *love anyway*.

Fire-Breathing Dragons and The Treasures You Seek

Renowned anthropologist Joseph Campbell observed that what most everyone ultimately seeks to experience in life, is the *experience of being alive*.

Truly experiencing *being alive* happens as we allow our false selves to die, and our true, authentic selves emerge to shine brilliant through our every choice, every word, every act, every day.

Intimate relationships are where our false selves often go to die.

That's one reason we do them, and the only reason they challenge us. Because in close relationship to another, we can first glimpse our false selves and we rarely like what we see.

Campbell researched and taught extensively about the fire-breathing dragons of European mythology. A dragon always protected treasure, such as gold or a virgin princess, some invaluable possession it could never actually do anything with. It never bought anything with the gold, and it never made love to the virgin, or ate her for that matter. It merely waited patiently, indefinitely, content to frighten off the occasional aspiring hero and then go back to sleep.

These mythological dragons were metaphors for the inner dragons that guard your own inner treasures. These shadow aspects of your being are what you must bravely face if you are to integrate your deepest truths and reclaim your wholeness, to live expansively in the fullness of your potential.

An intimate relationship quickly builds a formidable arena within which your dragons can be teased out of their dark lairs into the open so that you may finally confront them.

Confront them you must, if you are to ever wake up to the deepest truth of who you are.

Otherwise, without this self-awareness, you're destined to live powerless, a victim to the agendas and demands of others. Even if only in reaction to them, the world around you will decide who you are in any moment. For if you don't know who you really are, you will source that identity in the appearances of the world around you.

If you don't know who you are before you dance with a new lover, that lover's every move will define you. Their doubt will be your worry, their anger your fear. Their blame and disappointment will be your shame. Should they ever decide to leave, their absence will only beget your despair.

The human journey into self-awareness is discovering the brilliant, unique child of the universe you already are. Regardless what your intimate partner or the world has to say about it, you are an extraordinary being born to offer the full gift of "you" to the world.

So as you press deeper into the fight, besting every fiery beast you unwittingly project onto the face of your lover or their unskillful behavior or angry words, you awaken to discover the immense treasure of self-awareness: *how to love anyway.*

New dragons become less intimidating as you reclaim your wholeness. You learn to even harness their immense force for positive effect in your life. You stop depending on the unstable outside world to complete you. You're already complete, dragons and all.

Life begins to open up in ways we never imagined possible.

You come to know genuine happiness which Benedictine Monk, David Steindl-Rast, described as "that kind of happiness that doesn't depend on what happens."

You laugh deeper. You dream wilder. You love bigger, and you love anyway.

You are now touching the face of your true self as you wake up to realize you are already what you had been seeking in

TELL THE TRUTH, LET THE PEACE FALL WHERE IT MAY

an intimate partner: *You are brilliant, wild, authentic, radiant, free, strong, and absolutely unconditionally fearlessly loving!*

… but let's get ahead of ourselves.

Our Wounds Attract Perfect Partners

Why do you suppose young men so often love bitches and young women love the bad boys?

Could it be that partnering with people who are "bad" for us is actually a powerful pathway towards profound healing?

When I married a woman I did not know, my dragons began to awaken. It's no coincidence that I also began to awaken from the numbness of 10 years of stoic military living.

Our dragons are often reflections of psychic wounds suffered long ago, defense programs we installed in our minds, in our bodies, when some interaction with the world – perhaps with a parent or a sibling, a young lover or a friend – went terribly awry and we feared we might die. We made up a story to protect us from that happening again. We planted that story deep in our psyche, even into the physical cells of our bodies, where we would be sure to never lose it.

Through the unique pressure-cooker of intimacy, then, we unwittingly choose the partners most likely to surface those hidden wound-dragons so that we may face and ultimately heal them.

Author David Deida writes in his book, Intimate Communion, that romantic love is essentially the love of familiarity. Whatever patterns of loving we witnessed in our childhood, we grow up attuned to look for them in our adult partners. "Because romantic attraction is based on qualities in your partner that you unconsciously recognize from your childhood experiences," he writes, "you will be as fulfilled or as unfulfilled by your partner's love as you were by your parents."

So it isn't that we love people who are bad for us.

Rather, we unconsciously create romantic experiences that allow us to "continue the relationship we had with our parents and finally get the love we always wanted, the acceptance we always desired, the fulfillment that we always craved," writes Deida. However, "because we have unconsciously chosen our parents in our partner, we have chosen someone who will not give us what we wanted, in exactly the same way that our parents didn't."

In other words, we're attracted to the people who can best help us heal the effects of receiving incomplete love during childhood, a critical phase of life when we were entirely dependent on the outside world for both survival and identity.

Ironically, the "best people" suited for the role of helping us heal a lack of unconditional love may not be the most loving. Most of us don't love ourselves unconditionally because we saw our very human parents often not love us (or each other) unconditionally, and as children we naturally look to our parents to teach us what is lovable and what is not. Believing ourselves unlovable to varying degrees, then, we can't therefore often receive love from those who genuinely offer it. Deida points out, "our childhood imprint doesn't believe it is real."

Fortunately (or perhaps, unfortunately) contrast is a great teacher.

In my 20s and 30s, I ran fast away from kind women who knew how to love me well. I was drawn instead to harsher women I unconsciously knew wouldn't love me well, because I didn't love me well. My wounds demanded healing. Only a woman with a strong unconscious capacity for "bitch" was going to offer enough agonizing contrast for me to finally learn how to love myself.

We choose partners who challenge us and then repeat patterns of unhealthy relationships. We may also repeat the same conflicts inside the same relationship for years.

Because our wounds attract the perfect partners.

Until we learn.

Until we learn what's really going on we will continue seeking justice for crimes committed long before our current partner showed up. We will fling out hostile reactions like biological warfare to even their imagined offenses. (in a later chapter, we'll explore how all offenses are essentially imagined).

Our minds and bodies can hold subconsciously for a lifetime the memories of an early frightening experience.

Should a partner stumble across the hidden tripwire connected to that memory they may find themselves reeling from an ambush. Rather than fight the inner wound-dragon that just revealed its smoking nostrils, our frightened egos project the fight onto our intimate partner and we take up the battle there.

After all, it's far safer for a fragile identity, a false self, to look outward and blame another than it is to look inward and expose itself as a fraud.

We might say we're "just telling the truth" when we blame another for our upset. We might even be really convincing, with overwhelming evidence that they are indeed responsible for our upset!

Here's what really happened:

Our partner did or said something. Our wound triggered. Electric pain arced out from that unhealed wound like fire from a dragon's breath. As it rose to the level of conscious mind, it translated into vicious, angry, or merely critical thoughts that we projected outward through our mouths or behavior. We weren't genuinely rooted in the present moment, in what was actually happening. We only played out an elaborate mousetrap triggered by our partner's misstep which ended with their smoldering head in a basket.

When Valerie discovered my lie, she was understandably disappointed and angry with my choices. But the river of rage she unleashed for months, even years afterwards had its origins long before I arrived on her scene. Her emotional violence was fueled not just by disappointment in me, but also by disappointment she experienced well in the past, of which she was either unaware or simply unwilling to admit. In her mind, it was all my fault.

When we project our wound-dragons outward onto our partners and take up the battle there, we can do so much damage to the relationship.

Let's look at a few common wounds that surface in most relationships.

The Wounds We Project in Order to Protect

It's one of the most common laments in any relationship, and it takes many forms:

"You abandoned me."

In my work as a relationship blogger, author and coach (to individuals and couples), I hear the sadness and anger unleashed in this cry often. I've heard it from my own intimate partners, too.

One woman I had just started dating, got upset on our third date when she sensed I wasn't fully present to a story she was telling me. She was right. While she was talking, I had started calculating how I was going to get us across the street and into the theater I had tickets for. This theater did not allow late seating, and we were late. As we entered the lobby, she told me with a calm anger in her voice, "You zoned out on me. Don't do that again." In that moment, she felt abandoned and lashed out, trying to control my behavior so she didn't ever again have to face her wound of being left alone, or dismissed, or unvalued, or whatever still hurt inside.

That's the subtle end of the spectrum. On the other end, I hear from my readers and clients, from men and women both, abandonment stories of infidelity and even decades-long marriages that endure, but in which one partner mentally checked out a long time ago. Agony and upset and confusion and sadness reigns in the story, "You abandoned me!"

The angst unleashed by a partner's abandonment, whether their abandonment be real or imagined, subtle or massive, is but the pungent fragrance of an open wound suffered long ago. This wound is a consequence of our collective fear of death, of emptiness and aloneness.

I recall one day when I was maybe 5, I awoke from a nap in my bedroom feeling oddly alone. I called out with my tiny little voice, but neither mother nor sister answered back. Only emptiness spoke. Our tiny little 3-story suburban townhouse was quiet as the empty sky. I was terrified. How could they have forgotten about me? When they came home, I was a turbulent toddler mix of fear, confusion and anger. I let them have it!

I can feel that moment in my bones even now. I surely brought that reaction and its trigger into 20 years of adult relationships. If a lover did anything that even remotely resembled forgetting about me, terror would claim me.

We want to be full all the time: full of food, full of happy feelings, full of options, full of life, full of money, full of things to do. We fear emptiness, this aloneness like death.

The French philosopher Blaise Pascal said, "All men's miseries derive from not being able to sit in a quiet room alone." He said that 400 years ago, well before people even had smart phones to shield themselves permanently from solitude.

Until you learn to truly love yourself, to fully enjoy your own company and the emptiness that is your only friend when you are alone, you will fight doggedly against even the idea of abandonment.

When an intimate partner shows up and in a careless moment looks away and leaves you alone with yourself, your fear will trigger and throw out daggers of aggression. You'll communicate to this person, whether passively, stealthily or with great clarity and passion, that they better not ever again do that thing they just did … or they'll be sorry.

If your partner lacks self-awareness, they may respond from a wound that your demands are now triggering in them:

"Don't tell me what to do!"

The masculine essence in every human being is that which endlessly seeks freedom, autonomy, domination and mastery over things (while our feminine nature seeks connection, bonding, exquisite surrender). Our modern world has long valued masculine expression far more than feminine.

We prioritize independence (freedom) and self-determination (autonomy) over collaboration (the surrender of one's own will to a genuine love for the greater good).

Yet we're born powerless, absolutely dependent and unable to make any decisions for ourself, including even when to release our own bowels.

We can't feed ourselves, change our own underwear, ask for what we want, or even get up and leave when we don't approve of what's going on here.

Around two years old we begin to taste the thrill of doing things for ourselves. Our masculine expression kicks in when we start yearning to be autonomous, self-determining. This is also when the adults around us whom we depend on for survival start pushing back, frequently telling us, "Don't touch that!" "Put that down!" or simply "No!"

"Don't tell me no!" was a common refrain in my home as my strong-willed baby sister, 10 years my junior, moved through her feisty toddler years. She would snap those words at my mom, and my mom would snap them right back at her!

The excitement of learning to make our own way in the world, independent and autonomous, continues throughout childhood and into our adult lives if we stay adventurous.

We are therefore destined to know this inner conflict throughout our human lives, regardless whether we grow up with the most perfect parents, the most unskillful, or absent ones. In every moment of our lives, some deep primal masculine drive is urging us out of powerlessness onward into all-powerful. We are born to push our own limits, and the world is designed to push back.

When an intimate partner tells you what to do, it offends your inherent masculine drive, particularly if that drive is strongly identified with an ego, a false self, a false identity, that wants to believe it is already all-powerful. Your partner's direction also suggests that you don't know what you're doing, or that you did it wrong. "I appoint myself your guru-leader because you are weak, incompetent and powerless and I will show you the way," is how you interpret their command you didn't ask for.

You don't like to feel powerless. Your false self doesn't want to think of itself as weak and incompetent. So your little inner masculine toddler still learning to make his own way in the world perks his ears up and screams, "Don't tell me no!"

Your reaction has nothing to do with the other person making demands. Who cares if they order you around, or call you powerless or suggest that you're doing it wrong? Just because they issue instructions doesn't mean you have to obey them. Ever.

Still, your inner drive of powerlessness to powerful compels you to bark out, "Don't you tell me what to do!" It's ironic that this reaction to someone trying to control you is itself an attempt to turn the tables and control them instead.

Or maybe you don't try to control them by insisting they stop telling you what to do. Maybe you intentionally do the opposite of what they told you to do, in a desperate attempt to display the power and autonomy you obviously aren't even yet convinced yourself that you have. Or maybe you just check out into smart phone land, or work, or food, or TV, or sports, or shopping – anything to distract you from the powerlessness you know not how to escape.

Regardless how you respond, your partner's controlling behavior only reveals your angst of powerlessness and persistent dependency that you haven't yet made peace with.

Your reaction is also likely the reflection of a wound experienced long ago when someone you loved withdrew their love from you because you didn't do what they wanted. As your partner communicates that they need you to do something different, you're also hearing, "or else I won't love you."

The thought of the one person you want to love you more than any other withdrawing their love is terrifying, but only when you don't fully love yourself because you haven't yet discovered the brilliant truth of who you are.

If you really knew how extraordinary you already are, and how absolutely powerful you are to make your own choices at every moment, someone attempting to control you would barely elicit a raised eyebrow.

You would even have compassion for them. For you would see it's only their fear of powerlessness desperate to prove it can control something, anything, and you're the easiest target around. They're just screaming for attention and care, and they think if you give it to them they'll feel better.

And they might feel better for a moment.

My relationship with Valerie was a spicy mix of abandonment and control and powerlessness wounds all served on a crunchy bed of "You lied to me!" lettuce.

Being lied to touches on our most primal human fears.

It rubs at our sense of powerlessness. It's the cry of an ego terrorized by the ever-present uncertainty of the universe we live in.

When your partner betrays the certainty you entrust to them, your fear of powerlessness thrashes angrily. You are unable to accept that uncertainty is the truth of reality, and that you control nothing.

You blame your partner for their deceit, but you're really rebelling against this frightening reality of an ever-uncertain life. The certainty you entrusted to them was never real. Your partner is human and therefore susceptible to all the instability, change and challenges that come with being human.

Perhaps this provokes you, the idea that your anguished cry of blame, "You lied to me," is not really about your partner lying.

I'm not excusing lying – this is, after all, a book about living in truth. I'm also not suggesting that because life is fundamentally uncertain we should expect our partners to lie, or that we stay in relationship with them when they do.

I'm simply inviting you to explore how intimate relationships act as perfect divining rods attuned to reveal your unhealed wounds and fears. Your upset over a partner's lie serves to reveal your deep fear of this always uncertain world, and surely also your fears of abandonment, aloneness, powerlessness, emptiness, even death.

The world will always be uncertain; it may take you into the vast aloneness of death – or just your beloved checking their cell phone at dinner – at any moment.

The sooner you enthusiastically wrap your heart and soul around this unrelenting uncertainty, the sooner life just gets fun and the sooner you learn to love anyway. Expectations of what you think is supposed to happen next, that rarely does anyway, dissipate and all you're left with is the open spaciousness of this always magical present moment. You ease into the abiding state of possibility, wonder, fascination, with only the expectation of adventure.

This is the magical alchemy offered by intimate relationships.

As your intimate partners guide you towards acknowledging these wounds and you do the worthy work to heal them, your authentic truths begin to emerge more full-bodied and vibrant, like spectacular flowering plants no longer competing with stringy weeds for nutriments in the soil.

Can you see more clearly how intimate partners are gurus

masterfully (if unconsciously) guiding your journey deeper into self-awareness?

Yet Still We Lie

Still, it's no wonder we lie to intimate partners. Lying helps us avoid peering directly into these painful wounds like vicious gashes that run so deep into our psychic body.

I lied to Valerie because I instinctively knew there was something out of alignment about my decision to sleep with the other woman and it just didn't seem right to me; I definitely knew it wouldn't feel right to her. But I chose not to acknowledge my discomfort – and I was deeply torn in the days before as I considered whether to bring this woman to France with me. I chose to pretend everything was ok. My denial set us both up for massive chaos a few months later as reality smashed like an asteroid into the intimate world we had just started building.

Our intimate partners are perfect mirrors into who we are being and what we're avoiding. They may hold the very keys to our salvation, but not by simply giving us what we want or behaving the way we want them to.

When we don't get what we want from our intimate partners, if we can resist the brewing tantrum and notice that we actually are just fine without whatever we thought we needed, we take a masterful step towards reclaiming our wholeness. We can notice the world doesn't stop spinning, and we don't stop breathing or living a blessed, miraculous life.

We give them back the delicious freedom from being responsible for our happiness and put that job back on ourselves where it belongs (and where it always was, anyway).

Of course, we remain free to go get what we want somewhere else, or give it to ourselves.

> *You can have whatever you want, if you're willing to ask a thousand people.*
> – Byron Katie

Whatever path we choose, the partner we're with is exactly the partner we're supposed to be with, at least until we're no longer with them.

No matter how much we might protest that we're in the wrong relationship, until we take action and leave it, it must be the right one for us right now. For when it truly has nothing left to teach us, we can't possibly stay.

The Courage to Confront Our Wounds

The courage it takes to confront our own wounds is something the modern world doesn't prepare us with. That's because our world is afraid of its wounds. We get little or no intentional training that guides us powerfully into those seething places so that we could attend to them with understanding, with love.

Nope. We're thrown into adulthood with our basic math and history educations, cliche Hollywood story plots, and whatever relationship games we watched our ill-prepared parents play. Then we're expected to somehow magically thrive in adult relationships of our own.

It's quite the set up for mighty falls and all those divorces we lament as a society.

This book is the fruit of 20 years spent weaving in and out of intimate monogamous relationships in which I struggled consistently to speak and live my truth. Although the details of my struggles were particular to me, our head-in-the-sand culture sets us all up for this unending confusion.

My wounds have always been bullies on the playground. I could barely touch my authentic truths with those brutes constantly snorting their threats. They bullied both me and my romantic partners into believing thoughts of unworthiness.

As a result of all this ignorance, I've paid dearly in tears, heartache and disillusionment and watched my female companions pay as much, if not more.

It's my hope that reading this inspires you to look inside yourself for the answers to the clues your life and relationships are showing you. There's nothing wrong with your partner. You're with the perfect partner for you, even if they're lying to you, cheating on you, or outright abusing you. When you've truly learned the lesson(s) you entered that relationship to learn, you'll either remain or depart in relative peace. Even if it's abusive, you'll only leave when your partner's behavior has taught you enough about who you truly are to know that you do not deserve abuse.

The intense pressure of a painful relationship can eventually wake you up to the realization that you do have genuine value and worth as a human being.

You are choosing your partner. Every day. If you are uncomfortable in the relationship, there's almost surely a wound that obscures an unspoken truth. The reward of honesty, at least with yourself, is nothing less than freedom in your life experience.

When I did find the courage to express an honest, difficult truth with an intimate partner, it never led me down a path I regretted.

A relationship never ended with a woman I truly wanted to be with because of an honest, authentic and completely vulnerable truth. It always led to inspiring relief, deeper intimacy and better understanding of each other. It always led to an experience of my own rich fullness, because I discovered I could always stand tall in the authentic truth regardless whether my partner liked it or not.

I will only ever be truly loved for the man I genuinely am in this moment if I live openly the authentic truth of who I am in every moment. There is simply no other way. I have attempted the other way plenty, by not living in my truth.

Choosing to Stay in the Lie

If we're not willing to be honest and leave an expired relationship or accept the invitation to self-discovery, we will either slowly burn in the fire of unexamined discomfort or settle into the boring comfort of the familiar and silently ache for something to rescue us from what may feel like a living death. We might engage in all kinds of addictions as distractions. We might cheat on our partners, seeking comfort and stimulation elsewhere. We might focus on our careers or the children, anything to distract us from the quiet heartbreak of an intimate relationship that offers little true intimacy.

Still, many couples choose to stay in relationships where authentic truth isn't welcome or valued; it might even be considered dangerous when it threatens to upset the dominating beliefs at play in the relationship.

People who remain in such relationships where truth is routinely avoided often repress and eventually shut down their innate human longing for exploration. The unheeded desire for adventure is too painful to withstand for long. If we don't find the courage to follow it, we'll instead quash it altogether and steel ourselves for an era of relatively safe, if stagnant, routine.

I was constantly looking for validation, connection, and relief from outside my relationship with Valerie. The experience of a torturous intimacy with her was a disguised invitation to self-discovery, one I was not then willing to accept.

I looked to other people, women in particular, to be friendly towards me and assuage my shame and suffering. I wasn't seeking physical intimacy and didn't intimately touch another woman after my trip to France. I just wanted to avoid at all costs doing battle with the wound-dragons that this chaotic intimate dance was summoning from the darkness within.

In my ignorance, I blamed my wandering heart on Valerie's anger. Which just made her angrier.

By merely blaming the other for the cries of our unhealed wounds, we only prolong an increasingly dissatisfying relationship.

The longer we deny our authentic truths for fear of being abandoned or rejected, for fear of being alone or once again made incomplete, the longer we keep ourselves in prisons of our own making. We might even appoint our partners prison warden whose love, validation, resources, or good graces we so desperately seek. Naturally, they gladly take the job since they're unconsciously battling their own wound-dragons, too. You're perfect for each other.

The constant dysfunction that arises from suppressing our truth inevitably sows darkness and sorrow across the landscape of our relationships – and our entire lives.

Eventually, in the empty life created around such inauthenticity, we learn to reluctantly tolerate each other at best; at worst we lose all respect and willingness to even be in each other's presence.

If we leave an unsatisfying relationship and never touch the raw honesty that acknowledges our contributions to the failed relationship – if we resist the invitation to self-discovery – then we take our wounded truths unhealed into the next adventure. We leave, satisfied our partner's mine has been fully exploited of its gold, and maybe we decide there never even was any gold. Off we go, in hungry pursuit of authentic human connection elsewhere.

Eventually, we'll find something resembling the authentic connection we yearn for, for a time. Our new partner may even be living in ways more palatable to our tastes. However, we still need to discover the courage to connect with and live from our own deepest truths. Otherwise our newfound sense of exquisite connection will inevitably be obscured by the ever growing fog of our inauthenticity.

We can't escape our inner dragons. We can pretend they're not there, but then we miss out on the real treasure we seek. They'll remain buried deep in our psyche, always warding us away from the riches we came here to claim.

By slaying these dragons and learning to share our simple, personal truth in every moment with our partners, we give them the opportunity to meet us in the truth. When we mislead, lie, or manipulate to avoid our dragons, we dance the awkward, discombobulated shuffle of two strangers afraid to fully see or be seen by each other.

When we dance authentically with those who resonate with our authenticity, the dance becomes sexy and more effortless, deliciously unpredictable and adventurous. In the land of authenticity, relationships flow smooth like silk curtains embraced by the wind.

The Truth Liberates All Hearts

In intimate relationships where two people have been disconnected from or hiding their authentic truths for a long time, as one finally loses hope within the stagnant experience and confesses, the other may experience permission to open up and confess, as well.

In the act of confessing – and vulnerability is wildly sexy – they might find surprising congruence that unleashes exciting new rhythms in their relationship.

If they find their confessions expose a world of incompatible truths, better they know now, for life is precious and short and uncertain.

If you're genuinely not compatible with your partner – and you get to decide what that means – you're absolutely free to move on to explore other possibilities where your authentic expression in the world will be appreciated, even celebrated.

Otherwise, living disconnected from the truth just creates two lives: the one you're living, and the one you're aching to live.

As time passes, the psychological gap between the two grows farther and farther apart, and the stress on your inner world accumulates with it.

If you're lucky, reckoning day will arrive when life (posing, say, as a spouse) finally catches you in the lie or you just can't take the heartache anymore and finally decide to 'fess up.

However the truth gets outed, the earthquake roar of those two very different lives collapsing suddenly into one authentic experience can be deafening, depending on how long the stress of inauthenticity has been building. The sheer power unleashed in the collapse of a false life can send spouses and kids and bank accounts and homes and psychological well-being reeling into chaos.

If you're lucky again, you'll find your way through this dark night of the soul into a life of authenticity because you are just not willing to live the pain of living disconnected from your authentic truth again.

However, when intimate partners are completely authentic with one another at every step on the journey, there's little risk of world-shattering disillusionment.

A friend once told me that he only shares with his partner the "stuff" he's going through after he's clear of its implications. If he's still working out some inner challenge, something he can't quite make sense of yet, he'll keep it to himself and do his best to keep on as though nothing is up. I thought this wise at first, and I still do. However, if this internal wrestling match continues to linger, affecting our ability to be sincerely present in the relationship, confessing the confusion is essential.

The act of confessing confusion might be enough to resolve it.

In my mid-twenties, I had been dating a woman for about a year when I started to notice a strange experience arise in me. I had this foreshadowing sense that I was going to cheat on her. The idea kept floating through my thoughts like a dark cloud threatening rain on a day when I wanted to enjoy the sun! I had no desire to leave or lose my girlfriend; I did not want an open relationship. It was just a weird, persistent feeling that I might do something soon that would violate our monogamy agreement.

This feeling didn't try to justify itself with the idea that I was unhappy with my relationship (I wasn't) or that I needed some sexual variety (I was deeply satisfied with our sexual intimacy).

So one quiet Saturday afternoon, I nervously confessed my experience to my girlfriend.

She took my confession with mature grace and understanding, and we had an incredibly vulnerable, intimate conversation about our relationship. She also confessed she had been feeling strange curiosities about other men, though we both affirmed our desire and intention to stay together monogamously.

About two weeks later I went on a trip without her to see old college friends. I had an opportunity to have sex with a former college sweetheart. However, that strange compulsion had completely vanished from my body.

Somehow, by confessing to my girlfriend before any actual

violation of our relationship agreements happened, the tension of that inner experience melted away like an ice cube in summer sunlight. To this day, I believe if I had not shared my inner experience with her, I would have cheated on her. Then, my confession would have involved an actual violation and surely resulted in much more painful, tumultuous consequences.

Sharing my awkward truth with her, as scared as I was it would hurt her, turned out to be incredibly kind to both of us. It gave her permission to communicate some important thoughts that were getting in her way, as well, which created a deeper intimacy between us. Immediately after we shared, our intimate bond felt as strong as ever. Miraculously, the uncomfortable experience I didn't want to be having in the first place dissipated as a result of simply confessing it.

Telling the truth can be exhilarating, precisely because it often requires you out of your comfort zone, so disconnected and inauthentic is the comfortable norm of our world.

If you've chosen a partner who doesn't deal well with uncomfortable truths, then the journey together is going to either be treacherous or boring and likely swing unpredictably between both painful extremes.

We must either face the uncomfortable truths or live afraid and running from our dragons until we do, all the while forfeiting the delicious treasures they guard.

Marriage Only Sucks For Liars

Marriage gets such a bad wrap. Comedians and TV and movies and divorced uncles make marriage the butt of countless jokes.

If we were completely authentic with each other about our real experiences we wouldn't ever find ourselves en masse loathing our long-term lives together.

As children, many of us watch our parents do marriage like a game of thrones, as cunning adversaries. So we soon succumb to the practice of marriage as a long war of adversaries. We fail to realize that we are divine partners in this delicious intimate dance of primal opposites.

In our disconnected ignorance we may also get married under false pretenses.

People marry simply to feel better about themselves, to feel complete, to please their parents, to gain financial security, to distract from other wounds. When we're disconnected from our core truths, or simply hiding them, we're helpless but to live out our secret agendas. We suffer their smothering consequences, paying steep tolls in joy, peace, freedom to be who we are, authentic love, until we confront our own dragons.

Or we just bounce from one partner to another, touching the cold surface of the same lessons over and over while avoiding at all costs the deep plunge.

There's nothing wrong with skipping like a rock off water

along the surfaces of many partners over a lifetime. All paths ultimately lead us home to ourselves eventually, anyway.

When we awaken to the mysterious universe that lives inside our own heart, and in the heart of our beloved despite all we think we know about them, there is no end to the adventure of discovery.

When a relationship stops challenging us in interesting ways, or when we stop surprising each other, it's only because we're lounging in a comfort zone, settled into a static world view. We've stopped actively exploring beyond the boundaries of our current inner world and lulled our dragons to sleep by our pursuit of empty external rewards.

We've stopped telling the real, raw, authentic truth about our experience right now. Our world becomes static and boring, and so does marriage.

You're As Free As Your Willingness To Be Truthful

In her Monday night lectures in Los Angeles, renowned author Marianne Williamson would often say that the exciting, expansive love we experience at the beginning of a relationship is not merely an illusion to be distrusted, but a preview of what is possible when we finally learn to love another unconditionally.

Unconditional love is only possible when you stop making your intimate partner responsible for your happiness; when you stop projecting your wounds all over them; when you tell the truth about your experience in this moment.

Awareness empowers us to make choices.

Rather than living timid lives and refusing to face the dragons we fear, an intimate relationship can lure those dragons into the light of day and expose them for what they are – and they are us. We may have to battle them, but they no longer sit unseen within dark lairs silently driving us towards insane, self-sabotaging choices.

In the end, you are only as free – and your relationship only as satisfying – as your willingness to be truthful.

REFLECTION QUESTIONS FOR JOURNALING

Choose at least one question to explore:

1. What is your worst fear in an intimate relationship? Do you find yourself behaving in stressful / unskillful ways to prevent that from happening? How so?

2. What are your 3 primary wounds that surface in intimacy, that you project as anger, resentment, frustration or fear towards your partner?

3. Can you recall a time when you shared something deeply vulnerable with an intimate partner? How did you feel in the sharing? What happened?

4. Have you ever experienced an unusually challenging relationship? What role do you you played in making it challenging?

5. Consider that your most difficult relationship has been one of life's greatest gifts to you: what empowering lesson(s) did it teach you that make your life better today?

Part 2

Learning to Recognize and Tell "The Truth"

4

The Truth Changes

Consider yourself and your feeling right every time with regard to every such argumentation, discussion, or introduction; if you are wrong after all, the natural growth of your inner life will lead you slowly and with time to other insights.
– Rainer Maria Rilke

Nothing in life is permanent. Not even your truth.

Sure, it was true a minute ago. But in this moment, some new insight might have popped up that changed everything. A moment ago, your partner's persistent complaining had you disgusted, fed up, ready to flee. But you've just discovered that those complaints may point the way to a treasure of untold wonder.

Now you're a treasure hunter living inside a completely new reality.

How to Recognize the Authentic Truth

Whenever conversation with people veers towards the idea of

living authentically, consistently honoring your truth, I hear all sorts of objections:

My truth is often really mean.

Others could never accept or understand my authentic truth.

Sometimes my truth is just weird.

If I told my partner the truth all the time, we'd just have chaos.

If I consistently acted on my truth, they'd have to arrest me!

My religious book offers the only truth I need.

It does seem that our personal truths are sometimes in complete contradiction with social norms, religious ideas, even some laws.

But notice how this inner conflict routinely takes down homophobic, bible-wielding, monoga-maniac priests and politicians who scandalize themselves with male prostitutes and secret extra-marital affairs. The conflict they wage in secrecy between the strict religious-social truth they're proffering and some inner yearning that seeks out a particular experience proves ultimately unmanageable. They self-sabotage.

This self-sabotage is all but inevitable and happens to us all, if not in spectacular public fashion, when we attempt to live out of alignment with our authentic truths.

I've learned to recognize that I'm living out of alignment with some *inner knowing*, some deeper truth attempting to have its way with my life, by the sometimes unbearable discomfort I feel psychologically, emotionally, even physically. Something inside my field of intuitive knowing always seems to know what to do, what direction to move in, even if it doesn't make much sense to my thinking brain; even if that intuitive knowing is imploring me to do nothing or go nowhere.

Permission To Not Know

My mother gave me the best – though perhaps most challenging – advice when she said, "Bryan, when in doubt, do nothing." That gave me permission to honor even the voice inside that confesses, "I don't know."

Culturally, we really don't have permission to not know. Can you imagine a politician admitting that he/she doesn't know whether their ideas will work? Or two people getting married, exchanging vows that include "I don't know if I'll be the right partner for you for the rest of our lives."

Nonetheless, most politicians' ideas, unleashed upon a world vastly more complex than they can ever hope to fully understand, clearly fail to do what they promise. And according to the American Psychology Association, between 40 and 50% of US marriages still end in divorce, despite all the heart that goes into those poetic vows.

We place an incredibly high value on certainty in an always completely uncertain world. I wonder, if we were more comfortable to admit uncertainty, would we open a whole new frontier of possibility for our lives?

The illusion of certainty – because all we get is the illusion of it – allows the otherwise frightened ego to rest in believing that its ideas, creations, comforts, possessions and everything else that serves as evidence of its existence will still exist in the next moment.

So we daily fight to ward off the reality of uncertainty. We can't rest when it appears we've finally landed a comforting moment of certainty, because we know that experience of certainty is going to shimmer a moment, glitch twice, and then disappear like Princess Lea's holographic distress call, and then we'll be off on yet another anxious adventure towards another oasis of certainty.

The reality is we don't really know anything for certain. We can never know. Presidents don't know. Parents don't know. Your big sister doesn't know. That red-haired kid on the playground doesn't know. Scientists don't know. In fact, major scientific discoveries typically only lead to a whole new world of questions. Even scientific "facts" are based on an incomplete understanding of the entire universe. Much of our scientific knowledge rarely lasts more than a few generations before some new breakthrough upends everything we thought to be true and a whole new way of seeing emerges.

A brilliant music artist I once managed wrote a song called Plankton, inspired by the reality that we're living on a lonely giant wet rock hurtling through enormous space from source unknown to destination unknown. A March 2014 National Geographic magazine article about celestial black holes concludes poetically that we may very well be living inside one.

Some of our best scientists tell us our entire universe may well be one vast tangle of imaginary linty static.

Yet we dare think we know what's going on here ... for certain?

We literally have no idea how life ever happened, or why there should even be a universe to contain us at all.

At best, we're making guesses at everything, and each of us every moment are one blink away from oblivion. We can't ever know what's right 'round the next corner. Could be a sweet kiss. Could be an asteroid.

It's with awareness of this complete unknowing that honoring our truth everyday becomes fascinating. Indeed, if life is so unknowable, then it makes sense that my everyday truths would routinely change. Absolute truth cannot take root on a foundation of absolute uncertainty.

Why shouldn't my truth change constantly?

The World is Constant Change

The whole world is different from moment to moment. I'm not the same person I was literally 10 seconds ago. I just ate a flat, round doughy piece of delicious Indian paratha bread with a buttery sweet smear of Coconut Manna spread, something I had never tried before. It was amaaaazing. My culinary world just expanded. I also just wrote words I have never witnessed anywhere else before and just had a thought I had never thought before.

There are people all over the world right now thinking new thoughts (at least, new for them), seeing new things they've never seen, having new conversations they've never had, and lustfully devouring new foods they had probably even thought disgusting just moments before.

Countless new ideas and creations are being synthesized as thought worlds collide into one another all over the planet. Wildly imaginative scenarios are unfolding in this very moment, in actual reality, that would defy our ability to comprehend. Magical serendipities, fantastic inventions, confounding coincidences, impossible outcomes ... mind-blowing shifts in consciousness, perceptual changes, religious and spiritual awakenings ... all these things are right now taking place somewhere on Planet Earth.

Were I to witness any one of them, my entire world view would completely shift. All my dearly held "truths" could be upended at any moment!

I once read a religious pamphlet someone handed to me on the street; I can't remember if it was for religion or against it. It asked the simple question, "How much of all existence have you directly experienced?"

It was immediately evident to me that I had not experienced even 0.1% of all existence. In fact, in terms of ALL EXISTENCE and its infinite treasure of secrets, even the most adventurous human sponge has not soaked up in their lifetime even as much as 0.000000000000001% of all existence. Of course, I made that number up; I'm probably off by close to infinity.

What any one of us actually knows from direct experience is the equivalent to knowing just the slippery skin of a simple water drop in an infinite ocean of watery possibility. Our collective knowledge barely amounts to the entire drop of water in that same infinite ocean.

In other words, it's ok that our truth change from one moment to the next. Of course it will. As we become witness to some new reality we weren't aware of in the moment before, a sane, open mind expands to include this new possibility and embrace a new world view.

It's normal that a single new thought floating through your mind could carry enough gravity that your entire galaxy of thoughts rearranges to accommodate this curious new celestial body.

This is evolution in action: mind expanding to more fully understand an unfathomably vast universe.

An evolving, changing mind is the sign of a sane mind, one that continuously brings fresh awareness to reality as it unfolds anew in every moment.

Life Doesn't Respect Promises

We find it so often distasteful when people change their truths. We lambast our politicians for changing their minds, deriding them as "flip-floppers" among other insults. We hold the promise maker's feet over the fire, even when the fire has exploded and threatens to consume us all.

I'm not advocating for bailing on promises. Promises can come from an admirable place, when they're made in earnest. They're essential to the healthy functioning of society. Stop lights, start times and building codes are all examples of promises made between us that ensure a quality of living we wouldn't want to do without.

However, promises also tend to come from fear and obligation. The concept of a promise exists exclusively to set someone else at ease, to give them a sense of certainty, a confident knowing that the future is going to look as they expect it to.

I remember being crushed as a kid when my dad, whom I wasn't living with, wouldn't keep a promise that we'd see each other on some weekend. I never knew what was happening for him. All I knew was he told me on the phone that we would soon spend time together, and then we didn't.

Again, I don't promote failing to make good on a promise. I do believe there is a certain personal power in honoring our word.

Nonetheless, even when someone breaks a sacred promise – which is what happens to half the people in our world who go through a divorce – we can learn something profound about life, about ourselves.

Life doesn't respect promises. We humans made them up. Life lives itself in this moment. It doesn't bring the rains every season to water the crops. It doesn't promise the sun will shine tomorrow; clouds, a volcano's ash, a meteor, even our own death, might take the sun away from our eyes in an instant.

Life doesn't promise our parents will see us through to adulthood. It doesn't even promise we will reach adulthood. The only promise life gives us is that it will return us to the soil. It never tells us when.

We humans are lucky when we get to keep a promise.

At best, promises are a temporary suppressant but never a cure for the uncertainty that rules our world. We are children of this uncertain life and our ways are subject to this inescapable uncertainty.

The ancient Greek philosopher Heraclitus famously said, the only thing that is constant is change. That refrain has resounded through the ages, and we still proclaim its wisdom today. Yet somehow, we often fail to appreciate that our personal truths can change, too.

Nonetheless, change they do. Often in an instant.

REFLECTION QUESTIONS FOR JOURNALING

Choose at least one question to explore:

1. *Describe a moment when something deeply true for you suddenly shifted and a completely new truth emerged. Do you think that is possible for everything you believe is true right now? Why or why not?*

2. *Has someone close to you ever failed to keep a promise? How did you respond? Why do you think you responded that way?*

3. *Have you ever failed to keep an important promise? Why? What happened?*

4. *What comes up for you when you consider the world is inherently uncertain? Does it inspire fear? Does it bring you peace? Why?*

5

Your Truth is Simple, Only Your Cover-ups Are Complicated

If you tell the truth, you don't have to remember anything.
– Mark Twain

Consider that your genuine truth in any single moment may be as simple as the tiny black ink dot at the end of this sentence.

There it is, just sitting there, unconcerned whether you notice it or not, whether you act on it or not. You could read past it straight into the next sentence as though it wasn't there, though the resulting run-on sentence would sound awkward in your head. You could also imagine there are all kinds of other punctuations and colors and squiggly lines atop that tiny little black dot, which would surely have you scratching your head in confusion, bewildered at what you're supposed to do at that spot in the paragraph.

That tiny little black dot wouldn't be concerned about any of that. There it lives, content to simply be there and live its simple truth: this sentence is complete now. But you're free to ignore or complicate things as you wish.

You Are In Constant Motion

As we move through any given day, we make countless choices, we spend time in the presence of others or alone, engage in a variety of conversations and all kinds of physical and mental activity. We're constantly in movement.

Even when we're sleeping or doing nothing – or at least *think* we're doing nothing – our bodies are dancing at light speed, sucking in oxygen, ripping out its electrons and zipping them off on wild adventures throughout our connective tissue into neurons and across synapses; hormones squirt this way and that, cells replicate and cells die and get moved out by other cells through lymphatic tissue plumbing. Our bodies are little New York Cities, worlds that never sleep, making billions of miniature choices every moment that we're not even aware of, choices that endlessly seek balance and holistic well-being.

Stillness is an illusion. We are in perpetual motion.

Even our thoughts continually run rampant and only a few ever result in any externally visible action (thank goodness for that!). The most practiced meditators who succeed in focusing on breath alone for more than a few seconds nonetheless live with a monkey mind that loves to leap all over the place and occasionally throw its feces at curious onlookers.

Arising out of this incessant activity, this swirling vortex where physical substance dances with imagination, is what we each have come to know as a "me." This "me" is the grand collection of all that mostly unseeable activity. We're all just Humans Me-ing.

This "me" is in every moment a collection of everything happening right now within. "Me" is in constant movement. Every second it is making choices to move this way or that; in every new moment it is feeling this or that. It's saying yes, no, or let's just wait and do nothing but maintain status quo, in the face of whatever is arising in this moment.

Complexity only enters into our experience when we bring in these curious intellectual concepts called "past" and "future."

There Is Only This Moment

All negativity is caused by an accumulation of psychological time and denial of the present. Unease, anxiety, tension, stress, worry – all forms of fear – are caused by too much future, and not enough presence. Guilt, regret, resentment, grievances, sadness, bitterness, and all forms of non-forgiveness are caused by too much past, and not enough presence.
– Eckhart Tolle

When we allow our minds to wander deeply into "the future," one of humanity's primary indulgences, it becomes easy to create difficult choices for ourselves. Fear enters the game because we don't want to be wrong. We don't want to make a choice that leads *in the future* to mistake, failure, pain, unhappiness, etc.

But the future is an imagined fantasy taking place only in the mind, and mind is a master at playing out wild narratives. In this moment, the future does not exist. It's not happening. At all. Anywhere. Nor is the future likely to ever exist quite in the way we see it in our mind's eye.

Nonetheless, when our minds think into the imagined future, anything and everything can happen, and the worst of it usually gets our attention. Thus is born worry, impatience, fear, greed, etc; stressful emotions and states of being that completely overlook the reality of this exact moment.

Our decisions become immediately complicated as our simple truths get buried beneath a formidable avalanche of stressful thoughts fabricated by our own monkey minds.

The "future" we create in our mind is a fantasy founded on the stories of our past.

This "past" is also mostly a collection of fictions we tell ourselves repeatedly about events that happened prior to this moment, that in most cases didn't happen quite as we believe they did. It's one thing to make observations about what happened. It's entirely another to drown those observations in stories about why they happened. The world is far too complex, with infinite perspectives, for us to ever have a complete understanding as to why anything happens at all.

When I was three, my father picked up another toddler in daycare when I was his only child in the room. The story born of that moment was that I'm not worthy of love like other people. Taken into adulthood, that story convinced me that other people will eventually "pick up" someone else – another friend, another lover – once they realize I'm really not worthy of their love. So I'll do my best to be worthy of their love, shape-shifting myself this way and that, to stave off long as I can that awful, inevitable, moment of abandonment.

I am an old man and have known a great many troubles,
but most of them never happened.
– Mark Twain

We live routinely disconnected from present reality.

This fantasy of a future, something that doesn't even exist yet, influenced by fantasies of a mostly-imagined past, stirs fear within and guides the vast majority of human choices. We hoard for fear of scarcity tomorrow, even though few of us in modern society have ever experienced genuine scarcity in the past. We engorge on food, subconsciously concerned there might not be enough at the next meal, even though we live in societies that always have enough. We attack to be sure others don't attack first. Every morning, so many of us wake up and choose to prioritize the quest for more material wealth, thinking we'll feel better after we've gotten enough. We never do – not for long, anyway.

We constantly create convoluted moments of decision based on future fantasies and past delusions that dismiss an unfathomable number of variables. We get completely caught up in anticipating and attempting to control consequences which take place in a non-existent future conditioned by a largely imagined past, rather than allowing what's *deeply true for us in this moment* to effortlessly guide our way.

The Miraculous Present

When we bring ourselves firmly back into this moment – letting go for even an instant the frightening future playing out in our heads that has us unemployed, homeless, hungry, cold, pathetic and without friends or salvation – a glorious new world arises for us. It's actually not a new world at all, but the one we're actually living in right now. It IS glorious. No matter where you are, what you're surrounded by, or what condition you're in, the world around you is miraculous … if you just take notice.

A character in Jerry Spinelli's novel, Love, *Stargirl*, gives this beautiful advice to an eccentric, individualistic young teenager nicknamed Stargirl:

Live today. Not yesterday. Not tomorrow. Just today. Inhabit your moments. Don't rent them out to tomorrow. Do you know what you're doing when you spend a moment wondering how things are going to turn out with Perry?

You're cheating yourself out of today. Today is calling to you, trying to get your attention, but you're stuck on tomorrow, and today trickles away like water down a drain. You wake up the next morning and that today you wasted is gone forever. It's not yesterday. Some of those moments may have had wonderful things in store for you, but now you'll never know.

Today is indeed calling you. Patiently, day after day, moment after moment, the whole of your being is whispering the truth of who you are right now, in your fullness. It's telling you what very next movement would serve your entire well-being. Whether it's to go climb that mountain or simply stay in bed.

You're supported and loved unconditionally in ways you've never even considered. The entire cosmos conspired to make your life possible, right now. The solid ground beneath your feet supports you unconditionally. The sun shines down on your world without asking for a thing in return. The skin on your body, a space-suit perfected over thousands of years, perfectly holds all the pieces of you together, giving you the opportunity of a genuine lifetime. My comically insightful artist friend, Ash Ruiz, likes to say, "oxygen loves you so much that it enters your mouth and it don't even care if you brushed your teeth!"

> *Life is so simple, but we make it so complicated.*
> *– Confucius*
>
> *The best things in life are nearest: breath in your nostrils, light in your eyes, flowers at your feet, duties at your hand, the path of right just before you.*
> *– Robert Louis Stevenson*

The allure of embracing simplicity in this moment and the rich truths it has to offer is timeless. Simplicity is timeless. The promise of simplicity didn't disappear with the advent of the internet and smart phones. Simplicity is always present, like the absolute silence from which all sounds arise and collapse back into. Turn your iPhone off and put it in a drawer, and the awareness of simplicity returns, scary though it may be for a moment.

> *I am not a genius. I am just curious. I ask many questions, and when the answer is simple, then God is answering.*
> *– Albert Einstein*

This is where our deepest truths are to be found, in utter simplicity. With the most unceremonious simplicity, our own personal God is constantly whispering truth to us.

A Journey To Simplicity

I learned the hard way that my truth is always simple, never complicated.

A few years ago I started observing in the midst of uncomfortable conversations that I would start spewing complicated, elaborate sentences from my mouth like colorful magic ribbon from a magician's sleeve.

I was telling run-on stories, drawn out accounts of an imagined reality that avoided the simpler truths. As I woke up to this, I was shocked to realize I had for much of my life been weaving elaborate tales to avoid sharing the core truths I feared others wouldn't receive well.

I recently rediscovered a trove of old emails I had sent an ex-girlfriend over the course of a year, a woman I was both running away from and yet desperate to hold on to. My simple, if painful, core truth was that I just did not want to be in a committed relationship with her. I loved her, I was grateful for her, but I knew it was time for me to let her go and move on.

Instead of acknowledging that, letting go and getting on with living, what I wrote her over many months as I backpacked alone across Europe, through Egypt and India, over and down under to Australia, was an exhaustive novel epic detailing the endless subtleties of a mind utterly gripped by fear and confusion. This novel, which I crafted email by email, flew feverishly from my mind as it burned in the wrenching agony of wanting something my heart did not.

My thoughts were gripped by an awful fantasy future destitute of love and companionship, conditioned by a past in which I had never really known a deeply satisfying, enduring romantic love.

As I wandered through those old emails, I noticed how complicated my messages were, page after page after page. I recall one day in a sleepy Australian beach town, when I spent two long hours in a cyber cafe crafting one of my epic emails. After I had chiseled and carved and shaved and polished what I thought the perfectly balanced message to both keep her connected and still push her far enough away, I accidentally hit a weird sequence of keys that made my masterpiece tale suddenly disappear from the screen.

An electronic etch-a-sketch malfunction, my fantastic tale vanished back into my imagination from whence I had labored intensely for hours to extract it. I was distraught. I had just lost the illusion of control.

If I was sharing a simple authentic truth, it would have been easy to recreate.

Instead, I was tirelessly circling around a truth I dared not acknowledge, that I just was not willing to show up and be her committed intimate partner right now.

It was so simple! I knew it right then. My actions bore it out. My heart knew it complete. But fear kept me complicated, kept the simple truth buried under a picaresque mountain of beautifully constructed, heartfelt prose designed to do one thing: paralyze us both.

As long as I kept up this elaborate fantasy, that I "kinda sorta did" want to be with her despite overwhelming evidence to the contrary (I was on the other side of the planet with no plans of returning), I didn't have to face an uncertain reality. I sorta had the familiarity of her in my life while *sorta* having the freedom to explore what I wanted to explore at that time. There I was, standing in a desolate no-man's land of confusion and fantasy, mostly miserable and believing the alternative was worse: if I fully confessed my simple truth, she might stop loving me and would surely leave me.

I believed that if she didn't love me, no one else would show up for the job. I clearly wasn't ready to love me. Therefore, no one would. This was the horrifying immediate future scenario that played out in my head every time I thought she might slip away. I would be all alone, traveling the planet aimlessly, completely homesick for a home I could not find, with no one to love or care for me.

So I wove my tale like nylon netting and worked hard to keep her trapped in it.

To some degree I was successful. She stayed "in relationship" with me for months, allowing me to drag her psychological presence along on my travels without having to take anything else of her with me. But the effort I needed to maintain the fantasy and drag her along, combined with her obvious lack of enthusiasm for the situation, ultimately proved a burden too heavy for either to bear.

I never 'fessed up my simple truth to her, and our relationship ended abruptly one day while I was in Bordeaux, France, she in Miami. We were frantically emailing each other back and forth, when she sent me a message with the word "pathetic" describing our situation. That word crushed me. Because she was right. It *was* pathetic.

In that moment, I hastily ended the relationship with my next message, having learned nothing about telling the simple truth. In my own thoughts, I blamed the end on her characterization of us as "pathetic" and refused to fully explore why it had become so. She had thrown me a grenade with the potential to awaken me to a deeper truth, but instead I threw it back at her and took off running.

I had just let a year's worth of todays trickle down the drain, turning my back on countless wonderful adventures because I refused to hear my heart's patient whisper persistently pointing the way.

The Truth is Crazy Simple

It would be years before I got any awareness around my self-sabotage. It would take even more time before I had courage enough to do anything about it.

I painfully recreated this experience again in later relationships. I became quite skilled at spinning endlessly around uncomfortable but quite simple core truths. I was sure if I admitted to them, I would lose any precious external validation I was too insecure to lose. It was like doing the pee-pee dance while passionately denying I had to pee.

You can imagine the effect of this on the people around me, particular the women I dated.

The word "wishy-washy" featured heavily in one relationship. I hated to hear it, but she was right. I was paralyzed into non-action by my failure to accept what I knew inside to be true, and my ability to mask it even to myself with elaborate explanations. I could not move forward, held back by my inner knowing, but I could not withdraw, either, paralyzed by the fear of being undesired, unwanted, uncared for and unloved.

I'm 39 years old as I write this, single with no children. Although I'm still relatively young, the cost exacted from me in joy, laughter, mental and physical health, authentic companionship and love, as a result of not quickly embracing and confessing the simple truth, hushes me to stunned silence.

Fortunately, I now better recognize when I've begun lying to myself – and therefore to others – by how complicated my explanations become, and by how much work it takes to craft and maintain them.

The more complicated my sharing gets, the more I'm obviously avoiding an unsettling inner truth, creating instead some fantasy that requires acrobatic imaginative effort on both my part AND yours. I'm scared of present reality, which really just means I'm focused on an undesired future experience that isn't even happening right now and may never happen. I play make-believe in an imagined happy-place to avoid that outcome, hoping everyone else will hide there with me.

Thing is, I'm miserable in that happy-place.

More and more I'm discovering the crazy truth, that the simple truth is just that: crazy simple.

My authentic truth, in any moment, can typically be written down on one side of a small cocktail napkin like a great business idea: *I want this. I don't want that. I feel this. I think that. I like this. That hurts. That angers me. Yes to that. No to this. That pleases me. I'm confused. I just don't know.*

I have since discovered that I am always clear about what's true for me. Even when the truth is, "I'm not clear. I don't know what to do now." Even that is a delicious acknowledgement of genuine clarity.

Remember what mom said, "When in doubt, do nothing."

In this moment, I am always clear about what is true for me right now, about what I feel, want, believe, see. It may not have been true yesterday. It may not be true tomorrow. It may not be true for anyone else. But it is my truth right now.

Indeed, your authentic truth is always simple, even effortless.

Only the stories you tell to defuse its wild, untamable power are complicated and exhausting.

REFLECTION QUESTIONS FOR JOURNALING

Choose at least one question to explore:

1. Where in your life might you be spinning complicated stories today to mask a simple truth?

2. Where might you actually be hurting yourself/ others by not confessing a simple truth?

6

The Truth Does Not Manipulate

Truth without love is brutality, and love without truth is hypocrisy.
– Warren W. Wiersbe

One of my favorite parts about the authentic truth is it's never manipulative.

Yet we live in world steeped in manipulation! From intimate lovers trying to shame and passive-aggressive you into behaving differently to billboards that insist buying their product will finally make you feel good, it can seem like manipulation is the ocean in which we swim.

Manipulating is lying, playing with embellished stories and half-truths designed to make people think how we want them to think and behave how we want them to behave. We may not be doing it consciously, but that's what we're doing.

Our so-called "blind spots" that others see that we cannot are often the source of our unconscious manipulative behavior.

This is why self-awareness is such treasure. Only when we clearly see what we're doing can we make new choices.

When I'm engaging in manipulative behavior, my cunning survivalist ego is running the show. I'm the puppet master pulling your strings, expecting you to dance the way I want you to dance, for my pleasure. I might be telling myself, "This is for your own good." I might believe the truth will hurt you, and I don't want you to hurt.

Regardless how I justify it, I'm totally manipulating you for my own purposes.

What do I really know of your own good? Can I possibly know what you came to Earth to experience? You surely didn't come here to live out my agenda for you. Yet my strategic maneuvering (i.e. manipulating) is attempting to do just that: make you live my agenda.

It's the kindest thing in the world to tell the truth. Even if you don't wish it were true. Even if it might hurt another person (we'll explore how truth is never mean in the next chapter).

The Root Of Manipulation

So why do we routinely manipulate others?

Simple: we're afraid of not getting what we want or losing what we believe we already have. Whether money, sex, friendship, stuff, authority, or love. We manipulate to get what we want. We'll sacrifice our authentic truth for the taking of it, even if the spoils don't ultimately make us happy. In the end, what we're really searching for is relief, peace of mind, and we think pursuing all these things outside ourselves is the only route to having it.

Manipulating to get experiences like love or intimacy is a devil's bargain. Whoever's opening up to you is only opening to the fantasy you created. Until the authentic you is revealed, you stew in the brackish discord of your deceitful game. When the authentic you does begin to emerge, for we can't hide who we are for long, the inevitable disillusionment experience can be disorienting and often deeply painful for yourself and others around you.

When I was in fourth grade, I was painfully rejected by peers at school. The familiar pain of rejection I first experienced in daycare with my father was now happening at the hands of my peers. It was too much to bear. So I quickly taught myself how to play the game of getting others to like me.

As a teenager I became a social chameleon, existing between social groups to avoid the possibility of being rejected by any one of them. I would allow my wants, my vocabulary, my actions, my truths on display, to shape-shift in concert with the group of the moment. I was like a windsock swiveling at the mercy of the wind, constantly groping for its validation to puff me up and give me meaning. I did my best to subtly manipulate my peers' thoughts about me so they would accept me. I muted myself if I thought speaking up too risky, and I spoke up if I thought that's what my peers expected, even if I didn't really believe what I was saying – even if it meant rejecting someone my peers of the moment were rejecting. Better him than me. That's one way bullies emerge from otherwise kind kids.

Empathy: A Double-Edged Sword

A sociopath is an expert at tricking others into trusting them when their intentions are entirely self-serving. We all harbor in our minds a conniving little sociopath constantly scheming for the advantage: the ego.

The one significant difference between a sociopath and the rest of humanity is empathy. Our egos are designed to get us whatever needed for our survival, even at the expense of another's. They are not, by design, empathic.

Empathy, the ability to connect with and understand the feelings of others, is our collective saving grace.

I have always been acutely empathic towards others. I literally feel other people's pain in my physical body. I once almost passed out watching a friend get an IV inserted in her hand. Even the thought of it right now sends trembling waves of weakness shimmying through my stomach.

I grew up afraid of being rejected, invalidated, ignored, proven unworthy, disliked, unloved. This fact, along with an ability to peer inside what other people were likely experiencing in my presence, led me to take great care around others so my thoughts and opinions would not alienate or scare them away. I wanted people around me to feel good, partly because I genuinely want other people to feel good, but also because I believed that would make them want me around. Others wanting me around gave me the external validation I needed to feel good. It fed my ego.

I could almost always make the adjustments necessary to have others wanting me around. If I couldn't, and I wanted you to like me, I might be devastated.

For much of my young life, I believe I suffered from a rather mild but chronic depression. I had a difficult time laughing with my whole body the way it seemed other people could laugh. I couldn't really enjoy life to the delicious depths I was sure other people were experiencing. My own sister would thrill over a pair of yellow socks in a storefront window; I was envious and perplexed. I wanted to fully celebrate funky yellow socks, too. But that depth of joy seemed locked away from me like buried treasure.

I believe I lived inside this depression largely because I hid my authentic truth from myself and others.

My empathy for others gave me access to sensing what they were experiencing in my presence. My fear of rejection encouraged me to dance in whatever ways I thought would make them feel good. If I couldn't figure out which dance would do that then I'd shut myself down and stiffen up rather than risk making the wrong moves.

My ability to empathize with others became a tool for manipulating them.

This drive to manipulate can only be borne of a mind imprisoned.

Life Inside An Intellectual Prison

Since I was young, people often noted that I was an intelligent, insightful person. All my insights and deep thoughts came from a sharp intellect practiced in observing and then crafting beautiful insights about what I observed. I typically seemed to see more perspectives inside a given situation than what other people could see; it was both blessing and curse. I could easily win others' admiration with my astute perceptions, and this became my life preserver.

I wore my intellect proudly, arrogantly. I felt invisible in a room if I couldn't find something intelligent to say.

I was a brilliant teenager and then a wise young adult. I earned a Masters Degree in Human Relations and continued to develop big thoughts about humanity, our spiritual essence, what makes people do what they do, who we truly are, and what we're supposed to actually be doing here.

I had created gorgeous, inspiring intellectual frameworks around humanity's existence. As I experienced more of life and traveled the world, my ideas only got larger and more ambitious. Other people were awed by my profound insights, my elegant and inspiring philosophies, my capacity for observation and analysis, especially for my young age.

These insights and philosophies also formed the walls of my prison.

I was a passionate student of humanity. I wanted to heal humanity's obvious gaping wounds, the war, the famine, the greed, the destruction. After numbing military service as a rather reluctant Captain in the US Air Force, I was accepted into a Masters Program at American University to study International Peace and Conflict Resolution. I wanted to help bring peace to the Middle East. So massive was my void of validation that I felt nothing less than saving the world would fill it.

But when I left the military, I couldn't feel a thing. I couldn't cry, could barely laugh, couldn't get excited about much at all. I was only angry; angry at God, or whoever it was that put me through almost 10 years of oppressive military living (I later accepted that it was, in fact, me who did that). Now I was going to shake it all off, become a diplomat, and help bring true peace to the World – all an unconscious attempt to save my own soul.

I couldn't feel anything. It was like living inside a thick, full-body unlubricated latex condom. Wrapped tight inside my sterile intellectual philosophies, I felt completely separate from and impervious to the passionate, messy world outside that my whole being ached to experience. But I had so much of "the big picture" cleverly worked out that I was disconnected from my moment-to-moment embodied truth. Other than knowing that I wanted to save the world and figured formal diplomacy was the way, I actually had no real idea what to do with myself. I was low-grade miserable.

It took a long time to understand that my longing for so-called world peace only reflected a deep, sorrowful longing for my own elusive inner peace.

I couldn't tell anyone else the truth mostly because I couldn't hardly touch it myself.

Immediately after my military service, and before American University, I traveled the world, desperate to feel something. That's when I ran away from the girlfriend I couldn't let go of. She was my lifeline to feeling something, anything, even if – no, especially if – it was sexual. Sexual energy has always held secret pass-codes that short-circuit my intellectual security system.

Actor/Director Sean Penn moved me with something he said in an interview about his true story movie, "Into The Wild" [paraphrasing]: people will do anything to feel their life. They'll hurt people, hurt themselves, do crazy things, whatever they can to feel their life.

In my case, my addiction to impressive, intelligent thinking had created so much distance from my simple everyday truths that I could hardly see them anymore. I would unwittingly manipulate people in ways that impressed and sometimes infuriated them. People were impressed when my complex ideas enabled them to see a more intriguing world than they saw just a moment before. They were infuriated when they needed to hear my authentic truth, but all I could do was offer more intricately crafted ideas that danced around a simple truth I was far too horrified to touch.

So I remained in an intellectual prison, which caused great suffering to me. It particularly hurt women who engaged me in romantic relationships; for I would dance wide around my truth, manipulating them to not leave me, even when my own truth was silently whispering that I would soon leave them. They always somehow felt it in me, even as I did my unconscious best to not let them.

> *People say that what we're all seeking is a meaning for life. I don't think that's what we're really seeking. I think that what we're seeking is an experience of being alive, so that our life experiences on the purely physical plane will have resonances within our own innermost being and reality, so that we actually feel the rapture of being alive.*
> *– Joseph Campbell*

Our intellect routinely tells us we can't do things or create experiences that we can if we only decided to actually do or create them. It will tell us we can't afford to quit a job we loathe because we have to pay our bills when there are countless ways to create prosperity on this planet that won't trigger our misery. It will insist that boys shouldn't feel emotions or girls shouldn't like sex so much, thus creating generations of confused human beings distressed by the secrets lurking beneath their skin.

If we are to live everyday courageously in our truth, we must restore the intellect to its rightful place as a useful tool at the feet of our genuine enthusiasm. We must end the intellect's tyranny over our lives by ending its reign as our King and master.

Our intellect persistently tells us that it's got most everything in life figured out. It will tell us that life is either this way or that, and if we could just change a few things then everything would be absolutely perfect and we'd be happy and free.

Even that is a lie, if an alluring one.

Our Intellect-King would convince us it is wearing the absolute finest of invisible fabrics when it's just not wearing any clothes at all.

We live in a dualistic world. Despite our intellect's assurances that there is a destination not far from this spot where everything fits together and works perfectly in our favor, we will never live in a world without so-called problems.

There is no light without darkness. There can be no sky without ground. There can be no sweet without bitter. Every new solution only yields a new set of problems. We can only hope for a better set of problems tomorrow, never the complete absence of them, at least not for long.

But the intellect refuses to accept this and so keeps us ever-searching for a way out of confusion, which ironically just prolongs it. That's what I experienced when I left the military and wandered the planet aimlessly, desperate for an escape that my intellect could never find.

To Feel Your Life

This is the struggle to connect with our deepest truths, our authentic selves. We live in a culture that worships the mind, the individualized ego. We do not take good care of our bodies, which reflects in our poor stewardship of the Earth. We've become a culture that relies first on ego's truth, the loud, clever voice(s) that shape our thoughts and insist on what is true, rather than the deeply embodied wisdom that stirs in our hearts, throbs in our bones, but only quietly whispers its distinctive truth. Of course, that embodied wisdom only whispers until we've ignored it so long that it resorts to screaming at us in the form of physical or mental breakdown.

Our mind is essential. We wouldn't be human without it. It allows us to make sense of patterns in the world around us. It empowers us to actively shape the world in interesting new ways.

However, that same mind, which insists "I" exist separate from everything else, is ultimately only concerned with that which will preserve and entertain it. It's absurdly clever and only concerns itself with the body as necessary to preserve its existence and status of righteousness. As I said before, the ego is our own little inner sociopath. It's the full-body condom that works to keep us separate from the rest of life, sterile and secure in our otherwise suffocating little isolation chamber.

If our ego has to sacrifice the longings stirring in our heart to maintain the perceived admiration and validation of its ego peers, it will proudly do so. It will oppress our heart's desire until either it destroys every faint spark of it, or the pain of repression becomes so unbearable to us that the heart revolts and takes the body and ego along for a tumultuous ride of righting.

This is why we do so many things that defy even our own understanding and then mentally shame ourselves while lying about it to everyone else. We've given our sociopathic militant egos full say over an indigenous body-nation it barely understands and certainly doesn't respect.

In my case, trapped in my ego's elegant explanations of the world and disconnected from the wisdom of my body and heart, I was completely numb.

After living for years disconnected from the embodied truths stirring in my heart, I was desperate to *feel my life*.

When I left the military, intellectually brilliant and emotionally numb, I decided to travel to the most horrible place I could imagine in the entire world: Osweicim, Poland – better known as Auschwitz, the notorious World War II Nazi prison camp where millions of people died gruesome deaths in the grips of a human insanity, itself locked in an intellectual prison of grotesque character.

I thought visiting the grounds of this unimaginable horror would break the emotional logjam in my body and let me finally feel something. I didn't realize I was aching to break out of my own intellectual prison and connect with my deepest embodied truths. I just knew I needed to escape.

I only now see the irony of my pilgrimage to this notorious death prison.

I spent three quiet days at Auschwitz in Fall 2001, only a few weeks after the world's collective story changed dramatically on September 11. In that camp, I stood before somber grey stone wall, a speckled stage-backdrop hastily propped up against a larger red brick courtyard wall, where emaciated, broken prisoners were made to stand, bound and blindfolded, as Nazi firing squads took aim and shot them dead. I sat in green fields once fed by the warm smoldering ashes of tens of thousands of innocents murdered in a horrific gas-chamber death.

Because the 9/11 tragedy had greatly culled the throngs of int'l tourists, I was mostly alone inside this remnant nightmare of humanity's worst.

I cried twice in the museum, once near an exhibit displaying possessions ripped out of terrified prisoners' hands and off their bodies as they arrived at the camp: massive piles of tiny, ragged shoes, empty suitcases, toothbrushes, actual teeth, and more. I cried again when I read panels of exquisite, haunting poems and letters written by sorrow-filled parents to children lost in the horrors and soul-broken lovers to their missing beloveds.

Yet my tears never dropped below my cheeks. They were hardly cathartic as I was imprisoned in my own mental concentration camp, my rigid intellect, disconnected from the wisdom of my heart. My intellect would not let me feel the actual world. I was numb.

Over the next few years, it was only the destructive forces of disillusionment and heartbreak that began to crack my mental armor. Without apology or satisfying explanation, Life rudely began shattering my ego's expectations by completely denying the fulfillment of its various desires.

About nine months after Auschwitz, I abruptly married the French woman, despite the quiet whispers of an inner truth warning me against doing so. But I needed a woman who would refuse to meet any of my expectations, spoken or otherwise; a strong woman who would absolutely not be moved by the elaborate stories I tried telling her to make her act in ways that would please me.

I remember crying at the end of this short eight month adventure, in a movie theater, certain she was cheating on me. I was despondent over the rapid failure of my debut marital adventure, yet elated that I could finally feel something below my neck other than my genitals.

This was only the beginning.

A few years later, Valerie came along to help me continue the work. She was strikingly beautiful, intelligent, funny; in many ways my fantasy. Her attention made me feel worthy as a man.

She also refused to let me manipulate her with elaborate explanations. In fact, she was so loathe to be lied to or manipulated that even my legitimate truths were suspect in her mind.

However, she wouldn't kick me out before the demolishing of my intellectual prison was complete. She was loyal, a fighter. Since I didn't have the wherewithal to walk away from her intoxicating femininity, I stayed in this excruciating heart-grinder for years. As I wrote earlier, all my inner demons would be invited to this feast.

Despite her unwillingness to be manipulated, I still worked hard to disguise the simple truth in fabrics of fantasy woven by complicated and mostly irrelevant perspective. Very early in our relationship, even before she discovered my big lie, I noticed her rush to condescendingly judge me and certain friends for personal truths that didn't agree with hers. I quickly decided that much of my truth wouldn't be well received by her.

I was already practiced at disconnecting from and hiding my deepest truths, anyway, that it hardly seemed to matter. I really wanted this one. She only had to keep showing up as her fierce, sexy, brilliant self and continue daring me to tell the real truth about who I am.

She was the perfect storm for the destruction of my intellectual prison.

Manipulation Only Costs What You Most Want

Through years of recurring heart-break with Valerie, I began to see the hopelessness of manipulating another with complicated stories. I was once again desperate to convince a woman that I wanted to be with her, even though I knew so much misery in the experience.

In this relationship, I did my best to be myself while still also working to hide the real truth of my moment-to-moment experience. I was repeating the pattern: I couldn't bear losing her so I refused to admit that I was deeply disheartened by the dynamic and also completely unsure what to do about it.

Thus I dragged myself through another impossible situation.

As a few years went by, I worked tirelessly to manipulate Valerie into thinking about me in more favorable ways. I realized more and more that I had zero control over her thoughts or her happiness. She wouldn't be manipulated by my long-winded explanations that disguised simple truths.

I also understood more and more that I would never experience authentic love if I didn't confess the truth of who I am. Maybe she wasn't capable of fully loving the man I was at that time. But by working to manipulate and distract her with half-truths and obfuscating explanations, I never gave her the chance.

I only gave her a man afraid to be fully seen.

Working to manipulate her opinions about me ironically cost me everything I really wanted: authentic companionship, intimacy, love. That's what manipulating does. It keeps your real self hidden and costs you the deepest longings of your heart.

Isn't the person you want to be with the one who, no matter what they find out about you, chooses to stay?
– David Langer

If someone doesn't resonate with who you are, well, isn't it just the most delicious thing in the world to be with people who genuinely appreciate you for who you are today, which includes everything you've ever experienced and done in the past?

Letting go of the need for others to think about you a certain way or behave in ways that please you can be one of the most liberating experiences of your life.

What do you really gain when someone agrees with or validates you, anyway? A good feeling? You can feel good regardless whether anyone validates you. And if they leave, then you've been mercifully spared from living with someone who would not be able to fully embrace you, anyway.

You can always leave, too. Rather than tolerate someone in your midst who can't appreciate your full brilliance as a child of the Universe – or worse, who would actively seek to harm you – you can remove yourself from the situation. Eckhart Tolle reminds us that we have three choices in the face of any uncomfortable situation: "Remove yourself from the situation, change it, or accept it totally."

In some cases, the clear choice is to remove yourself. In other cases, it may be to stand your ground and work diligently for change. I'm certainly not an advocate for sitting idly by while the world around you acts in insane ways that cause real damage.

Although I'm addressing mostly personal relationships in this chapter, these ideas powerfully inform our capacity to live authentically in our professional worlds, too. If I have to deceive and manipulate people to make them buy my product, service, idea, etc., then perhaps it has little genuine value to the world and I'd do better to create a different product.

Whether personally or professionally, it's the easiest thing in the world to let other people think whatever they want to think.

Those who resonate with who you authentically are and what your authentic being has to offer will be attracted to you. Those who don't, won't.

Why would you want to manipulate yourself and others to be around those that can't appreciate the authentic you, anyway?

REFLECTION QUESTIONS FOR JOURNALING

Choose at least one question to explore:

1. Where are you working hard to get others to think or behave differently simply to validate you? What might happen if you relaxed the effort?

2. What do you think would happen if you gave up trying to convince anyone of anything and simply gave them freedom to think, believe, do whatever they chose?

3. How do you use your intelligence – ideas, philosophy, perspectives, well thought-out stories, etc. – to mask your simplest truths? What might this really be costing you?

7

The Truth is Never Mean

You don't always have to chop with the sword of truth.
You can point with it, too.
– Anne Lamott

The truth is absolutely never mean. Never.

No matter what you might think about it. If it's your genuine truth and not some insane judgment you're vomiting into the world, then even the most difficult truth you might have for another is the kindest thing in the world.

If we're going to make any real progress towards living a life in alignment with our authentic truths, we must explore the difference between those authentic truths and the insane thoughts we regularly have about the world, other people, and even ourselves.

Yes, you have insane thoughts. Every day. You often believe them. And they can be quite mean. But they're not true.

Let's dive in.

Our Inner Asshole

When I first started dabbling in consciously telling "the truth" some years ago, I thought it meant that I had to say everything on my mind. If I thought you a jerk, I should just say it. If I wanted to have sex with you, I should just say it. If I thought your work crap, I should just say it. Steve Jobs apparently practiced that philosophy, proudly so, and he built Apple. But Steve Jobs was also an asshole, and he admits as much in his officially sanctioned biography.

An asshole, for the purpose of this exploration, is one who takes perverse pleasure in emotionally and psychologically tearing other people down.

Of course, no one human being can be completely labeled an asshole. Rather, each of us has an "inner asshole" whose truth only looks outward and believes in its cynical judgments. That inner asshole also lacks empathy (it's a bit sociopathic that way). It insists the outside world immediately change to its satisfaction or stand naked and weeping in the harsh glare of its cold judgment. Some of us manage that hot-headed little gremlin asshole better than others. A lot of us don't manage it at all, giving it free-reign to run our mouths and make ill-advised decisions.

There's a twist.

While I don't condone asshole behavior, that nasty little gremlin is essential to human evolution.

As an asshole gremlin takes over its human host, poking its

finger in other people's faces (and usually back at its own face, yours), accusing others of being ugly, stupid, worthless, incompetent, etc. it offers an incredible opportunity for those recipient people to experience what is actually not the truth about who they are.

Experiencing the stark contrast of what is not true about who you are can be an essential step along the way to discovering what actually is the truth of who you are.

"What?" … you may be thinking.

I'll explain.

Shit Makes The Flowers Grow

With awareness of what's really going on beneath surface behavior, we can empower ourselves to grow more psychologically, emotionally, even spiritually functional when exposed to other people's gremlin dysfunctions.

For example, stewing for years in the face of Valerie's incessant criticisms gave me ample time to explore her angry stories about me and confront the demons within me who clearly agreed with her. Her words, brutal as they often were, brought me face to face with my deepest fears: that I might actually be unworthy and unlovable.

It's tempting to think our relationship would have been better had she focused on the best in me instead of the worst. Perhaps it would have been. Regardless, her proclivity towards criticism and condemnation gave me the most incredible opportunity to explore and ultimately discover for myself that all those negative, critical thoughts I also believed about myself … well, that they just weren't true.

As her intense critical nature met my fear of rejection, I stewed in that excruciating conflict for a few years. The light of awareness eventually revealed that I was none of those nasty things she was so often yelling at me. Yes, I was out of integrity in many ways, and her criticism was an invitation to confront those blind spots. But I wasn't "disgusting" or "pathetic" or "unlovable" or "a horrible person" – all words that her inner asshole gremlin hurled at me throughout our relationship.

She attempted to shame me over and over again in even more creative ways than these. I tortured myself by agreeing with her in my own mind. But the light of awareness gave me the sweetest gift of being able to confront those asshole gremlins in my own head and question them all.

Although I went through a very dark time, this proved to be one of the biggest transformational experiences of my life. I had to confront unhealthy behaviors which were always supported by self-defeating thoughts. Valerie served as a surrogate fire-breathing dragon who battled gallantly to scorch my self-deprecating false-self beliefs in the cauldron of her own wild fury. I made her the enemy, when she was my biggest ally.

As an aside, you're surely noticing by now how deeply I dip into the well of my intimate relationships as a rich source of profound lesson. The journey to courage in living our authentic truth can only take place in relationship to something that would otherwise prevent us from living so: family, community, friends, circumstance, intimate relationships, and of course ultimately our own selves. In my case, women have been significant teachers for me on the journey into fully living my own truth. I am profoundly grateful for every woman I have ever shared an intimate relationship with, as so much of the Man I've become and am still evolving into is due to their presence in my life.

One of my early crazy experiments in relationship involved consciously letting my inner gremlin speak its unfiltered truth. As I allowed myself to verbally vomit every thought out of my head, I quickly discovered that a lot of my thoughts were not based on any deep, genuine truth. They were just insane thoughts standing atop other insane thoughts, like a giant Jenga thought-puzzle poised to topple over at the slightest investigation.

As I looked closer, so many of the thoughts I set free with my mouth either offered no meaningful contribution to a situation or just unnecessarily hurt people.

This particular lesson really began in my relationship with the French woman in Bordeaux. She had no problems speaking her simple, unfiltered truth to me.

She was so forthright with her thoughts that her sentences would smack across my face like a barbed whip. As an American who had grown up in a far less forthright culture than my new French wife did, her propensity for hurling jagged-rock thoughts at my forehead began to teach me firsthand the meaningful difference between being honest and just being mean.

Mean Is A Matter Of Perspective

The idea of "being mean" is a slippery slope, since another's words only have the power we give them to make us feel either good or bad. Take this "don't be mean" paranoia too far and all of a sudden we're turning everyone into powerless victims whose fragile self-esteem needs constant massaging and caressing. As I wrote earlier, even the unkind words from someone else's inner asshole can ultimately serve us with the powerful contrast of experiencing what we are NOT so that we may deepen our awareness of who we truly ARE.

Let me illustrate with a fun, personal example.

Have you ever cursed someone out (or been cursed out by someone) in another language you are not fluent in? I did once. To end an awful argument with my angry french mother-in-law, I told her, "Tu me fais chier!"

Mean anything to you? Yeah, pretty much me neither at the time.

I only spoke that phrase because I had recently learned that those sounds strung together create an insult guaranteed to make a french person choke on their croissant. Which is pretty much what I wanted to do, metaphorically speaking. I just wanted to end the argument.

But maaaaaaan when I set those curious sounds loose from my mouth they must have gone and done a war dance on her ear drums. You would have thought I spat napalm onto her face! What was a tiny smoldering brush fire suddenly exploded into a massive world-on-fire conflagration! My now infuriated FMIL (French mother-in-law) cocked her head severely at me and unleashed a thick crackling column of red, orange and blue dragon breath fire that scorched me burnt marshmallow black.

If you and I were arguing and I said, "Tu me fais chier," unless you speak french you would just think I was having a stroke and making baby talk. Those sounds could unleash no emotional charge in you because your mental dictionary has no entry for them. Even if I screamed it with intense energy, my eyes and veins popping out of their rightful places on my body, you would probably just be perplexed, wondering if I were possessed by a demon speaking some ancient language. You would surely react to the force of my body language, but you would have no intellectual story attached to the sounds coming out of my mouth.

Words, in and of themselves, have no power to make you feel a certain way, unless you intellectually agree to let them do so.

The direct translation of "tu me fais chier" is "you make me shit."

Yeah, I know.

That's nasty. Sometimes the truth clawing up my throat is just nasty.

Here's the surprise twist:

I've come to realize that in angry, agitated moments, my so-called truth is usually nothing more than an unquestioned judgment, an unquestioned thought – the kind that insists without reflection that something or someone should be different than I currently perceive them to be.

Allowing this unquestioned thought to speak – giving the reigns to my inner asshole – is like vomiting my sickness all over the room. Or in the case of my mother-in-law, dumping my kaka all over the place and blaming it on her, which is exactly what an inner asshole would do.

I've never met anyone who genuinely enjoys being told they should be different than they are. I didn't like it when FMIL was saying so to me. She clearly didn't appreciate it from me, nor did her daughter who arrived home a few hours later. Not one woman I have ever known has appreciated even the slightest hint from me that she's not ok as she is right now, nor has any friend I can recall. My adversaries – in athletics or otherwise – may have thrilled on it, but only because it gave them more incentive to step up and whoop my ass.

Even constructive criticism usually isn't appreciated unless it's invited. Sure we all have room to grow – most of us LOTS of room – but few people appreciate unsolicited suggestions about where or how that growth should take place. Even fewer of us enjoy being told we're bad human beings.

"You're incompetent."

"You're a jerk."

"You're stupid."

"You're mean."

"You're ugly."

"You're not right for me."

"I don't enjoy being around you."

"You bore me."

"You should be different than you are."

"Tu me fais chier."

No doubt you've held some variation of these thoughts in your head while aching to spit them at someone in front of you. I have. And I've spit them out, as you surely have.

While we constantly say such things in our own heads, blurting them out loud does not yield the peace of mind, joy and contentment we so deeply crave. Although the brusque French might disagree with that conclusion, I was married to a strong-minded, free-mouthed French woman and I assure you she was quite far from the most contented, joyful person I've ever met.

If joyful contentment is a desired experience for you, simply vomiting your arrogant judgments all over people is not a recommended practice.

You can be right, or be happy.
– Gerald Jampolsky

Vomiting out these kinds of judgmental truths only leads to emotional barriers erected between people, which inevitably leads to deceit and dishonesty. It definitely got me kicked out of my charming, historic Bordeaux centre-ville apartment ... forever.

Once someone knows that you think they should be different – if they're attached to having you in their life or simply having you think a certain way about them – they're going to do their best to show you the thing you want to see in them, even if it's a complete lie. Either that or they'll counterattack and find something about you they think should change.

Thus the war is on. Everyone eventually loses this war, even when we win.

You can't really place blame 'cuz blame is much too messy,

some was bound to get on you while you were trying to put it on me.
– Ani di Franco in "Hour Follows Hour"

This may be a tough concept to get your thoughts around. You may be scratching your head, thinking of obvious examples in your life where this just doesn't hold up. There may be situations in your immediate experience, someone who really deserves all the verbal violence and vitriol coming to them, that you're just absolutely *certain* are true. No amount of clever metaphor or philosophical gymnastics is going to change your mind about it.

I struggled with the same, and still do sometimes.

So what do we do with those sticky, jagged gobs of chunky truth-meat that only scratch and claw at our tender throats when we choke them down?

What do we do with those judgments that persist on insisting my dad really *is* arrogant and condescending!? My partner really *is* an inconsiderate jerk sometimes!? My girlfriend really *does* look fat in those pants!? My french mother-in-law's presence literally *does* roil my intestines!?

The World Is Your Mirror

I wasn't able to really begin moving these challenging ideas out from my head and into actual living until I discovered "The Work" by author Byron Katie.

Katie's first book, *Loving What Is*, introduced the notion of questioning stressful thoughts; all those ideas, beliefs, perceptions, opinions, etc. that continually reverberated through my brain that just seemed to cause me discomfort, regardless whether they were true. (I won't go specifically into her content here; I recommend you discover Katie's work for yourself at thework.com or search youtube.)

Katie's simple process to question my angry, stress-filled thoughts gave me unprecedented insight into how every judgment I made about anything was only a fictional story I believed in my own head. Sure, the story might be based on some observable facts. But like a world class chef who can make a sumptuous 12-course meal out of a piece of broccoli, I discovered that I routinely dunked bare facts in rich saucy meaning of my own making to create a whole new experience that barely resembled the original piece of broccoli.

Additionally, Katie's inquiry revealed in a grounded, tangible way that every judgment I made only reflected, like a perfect mirror, me.

The world is my mirror. I am what I passionately judge others to be.

This idea was revolutionary to me.

Every angry, pissed-off, arrogant or resentful judgment about the world outside myself and anyone in it only points to something in me that perfectly mirrors that external thing I'm so upset about. In other words, your arrogance can only upset me by triggering my own arrogance.

Initially, I rejected that idea as stupid.

I had big ambitious ideas about how the world and people work that seemed to hold up. I could clearly see all that was wrong with the outside world and what we needed to do (or be) to fix it. When an obvious injustice triggered my disgust, no way I was going to accept that injustice as reflecting an equal injustice I was somehow committing myself. I truly believed myself capable of only helping the world, not contributing to its perversion.

One day, while still struggling with this idea, I was sitting with a friend who was reacting angrily to news of a child being murdered. In discussing this "world is my mirror" idea, he refused to accept that his angry, emphatic judgment that it "should not have happened!" pointed somehow to violence in him that would make him hurt a child, or anyone for that matter.

I understood his objection. It seemed a solid refutation of the idea. I despised my father's obvious arrogance and I was just certain there was no way I was arrogant like him. Still, this idea wouldn't let go of me so I went home and meditated, trying to find my way inside it like a secret passageway whose trigger switch must be somewhere in the grande library.

Late that night, while I lay in my bed staring at the ceiling, it popped.

It hit me that perhaps my friend wouldn't do actual violence to a child, but he would do violence to that violence. He would, with violence emanating from his own being, exterminate the world's violence. I saw it in his poorly veiled rage when he spoke about the incident.

It swept through my awareness like a tsunami: only my arrogance can have a problem with my dad's arrogance. Only if I judge negatively can I have a problem with another who judges negatively. Only my ego can have a problem with someone else's ego (or even my own ego). Only my inner aggressor can tell someone else's aggression to "suck it!"

My mind was blown open. Suddenly, any so-called "truths" I held that insisted the world outside me be different were nothing more than clever stories at best and outright lies at worst, all masquerading as thoughtful insight.

It almost became a game at that point, to hear my awful judgments about others and explore how they pointed to the same experience in me.

It didn't mean I suddenly condoned violence or arrogance or difficult French mothers-in-law, but I did begin to see how my angry judgments of such things were clever coverups for an experience within me that I wasn't seeing at that moment.

All of a sudden, the entire world around me no longer

loomed dark and foreboding with sinister monsters everywhere scheming to snuff out my life.

Instead, everything was immediately replaced by guides and gurus all pointing to the dark, wounded aspects of my own nature I previously refused to acknowledge, and so could not heal.

Now, whenever I feel discomfort inside me that wants to blame some external reason for its existence, I know there's something deeper at play. I know that bothersome external thing is somehow only mirroring the same bothersome thing stirring within my own being. The connection isn't always obvious, and sometimes the best I can do is simply acknowledge the pain I feel without understanding why it's being triggered. But at least I know better now than to outright blame the world around me for it.

This always fresh orientation frees me to live in and fully love this world as it shows up in every moment, even when it shows up crazy, which it often does.

Remarkably, because I'm no longer so upset or discouraged by all that craziness I still see happening around (and within) me, I laugh a whole lot more. Life has become much more entertaining. That the world is my mirror has been one of the most liberating and entertaining insights of my life.

Granted, this discovery hardly made my judgments go away. My actual awareness of this insight still waxes and wanes as life pushes and pokes me every day. I still routinely think snide, disgusting thoughts about other people, wishing they would either change or go away so I could have peace of mind. I could spit those thoughts out as the best truth I've got in this moment. But it does stay close to me, that if I'm telling you with ugly enthusiasm, "Tu me fais chier!" most likely at that moment, I'm making you shit, too!

I am no longer interested in living amidst so much kaka.

The Kind Truth Can Still Hurt

Sometimes we must confess difficult truths that will hurt other people. If you've ever ended a relationship, the kindest way to do it is simply be honest. That doesn't mean necessarily offering your specific reasons for leaving, which may not be appropriate or helpful. In the end, the kindest truth you can share is that the relationship no longer serves you, and that you're clear about that.

Years ago, in the very early days of online dating, a woman wrote to me with interest. I was going through a radical truth experiment at the time, and so I thought I would share with her why I wasn't interested. I believed it would serve her in some way, and that she would appreciate my honesty. So I wrote, with sincerity and warmth in my tone, that although she was clearly an amazing soul, I wasn't interested because I was attracted to thin women. I assured her there were amazing men out there who would love her for the full-bodied woman she was.

I hit send.

Within minutes, I received a reply with such vitriol and hate that I started to shake. For the next month, she stalked and threatened me with violence, revealing that she had found out where I lived and that I was in actual danger. She had not appreciated my honesty. And I soon grew to appreciate that what I had done was, indeed, completely unnecessary.

That might seem like an easy one, but what about more subtle situations with people we're already in relationship with; people who we think need to hear our truth if anything is going to change for the better.

There is a big difference between criticizing your partner and merely confirming that, actually, you did not enjoy her proud experiment of potato ice cream radish pie.

Sometimes what we authentically want to say is indeed going to hurt someone we don't want to see in pain. Even if we've sincerely determined that we're not coming from an angry, spiteful place, it still might hurt. In this case, we need to ask ourselves at what cost do we remain silent.

Am I costing myself joy by remaining silent? (Am I willing to eat awful pie for the rest of my life because I'm not telling the truth?)

Could my silence prevent another from getting important feedback they need to live the life they want? And are they asking for my feedback?

If they aren't asking for my truth, am I just trying to meet some unmet need of mine that isn't their responsibility to meet? Do I just want to feel significant? Valued? Loved?

These are valuable questions worth asking yourself to check in on whether it's actually necessary you offer your authentic truth to another person. Sometimes, silence is kind. Silence can be a powerful expression of authentic truth, as well.

Whether we choose to speak or stay silent, we live in a friendly universe.

Byron Katie wrote, "Nothing happens to us; everything happens for us."

We can all grow more functional through repeated exposure to each other's dysfunctions. Even what we would perceive as "mean" can serve our evolution as thoughtful human beings – if we allow it to.

To really understand, not just intellectually, but in your whole body, that the authentic truth is never mean, you must learn to take full responsibility for your own aggression, arrogance, rudeness, lack of courtesy, condescension, etc.

As you explore deeper the possibility that the world is truly your mirror, you can discover the truth about your negative judgments and crazy thoughts as insanity built atop fantasy. Your entire experience of the world can transform.

Meanness will essentially cease to exist for you. Where it once loomed before you menacing and vengeful, you now quickly recognize it as frightened confusion and ignorance. In other words, meanness becomes innocence.

Or as that wise dude, Jesus, once reportedly said: "Forgive them, for they know not what they do."

REFLECTION QUESTIONS FOR JOURNALING

Choose at least one question to explore:

1. Think of something about the world that really angers you. Would you rid the world of that if you could? Notice your reaction. Do you feel anger or frustration arise in your body? Can you find how that external experience points to something in you that is not yet at peace? (note: this isn't about condoning injustice; it's about simply noticing how bothersome external experiences often point to unease in our own internal world)

2. Recall a time when telling your truth apparently hurt someone. Were you genuinely communicating an authentic personal truth? Or were you making a critical judgment about how they should be, do, think?

3. What does your "inner asshole" get mad about? How do you treat other people (or yourself) when this little gremlin is running the show?

8

The Profound Kindness of Truth

> *The truth is the kindest thing we can give folks in the end.*
> *– Harriet Beecher Stowe*

Telling the authentic truth means I share with you the world as I see it, what I'm experiencing, what's real and true for me. That in turn empowers you to dance with me – or not – in the ways that feel best to you and most honor your authentic truth.

That seems infinitely kind to me.

If I tell you yes when I'm aching to say no, you're stuck with someone whose heart isn't truly into the yes, and I'm stuck living disconnected from my heart's deepest longing. Even if my thoughts tell me it would be more kind to you to say yes when my heart says no, this doesn't serve either of us.

Although that certainly does create the foundation for a powerful lesson! We silly humans sure have a curious propensity for teaching ourselves with self-inflicted suffering.

Ironically, we inevitably discover that one of those great

lessons is that it plain hurts when we don't live our authentic truth.

Why not just confess and live it from the start?

Layers Of Truth

I don't yet have children, but I was listening to a podcast the other day about the sacrifices parents make in the name of "showing up" for their kids. One particular story told of a man who would attend his high school daughter's every musical orchestra performance, which happened monthly during the school year. As the story progresses, we learn that the man was often deeply bored at these recitals. He would track the creeping passage of time by checking off in pencil in the program each song as it was played, fumbling high-school interpretations of "America, The Beautiful" and "Feliz Navidad," thus noting a slow but undeniable progress towards each concert's merciful end.

Our authentic truth often has multiple layers. From a certain perspective, these concerts are not the father's idea of time well spent. The music can be awful and unoriginal, and it typically takes place in sterile, drab high school auditoriums. But at a deeper level, this man clearly relishes being in the same room with his daughter as she expresses the musical inspiration flowing through her, regardless how malformed it may still be. The joy he directly experiences by knowing his daughter feels supported and loved and seen by her father, far outweighs his discomfort with every missed beat.

His deeper truth brings him to those auditoriums repeatedly and enables him to sit through what is otherwise an unpleasant experiences. He could focus on a different layer of truth, the one of his discomfort, which would also be genuinely true. But then he'd miss out on his deeper yearning to simply show up for his daughter.

Imagine if the deepest authentic truth he could connect with was that he could not bear those recitals, that the pleasure his daughter gets by seeing him in the audience was simply not enough for him to willingly show up.

Would it be more kind for him *not* to be there, if he is only now capable of resenting his choice to show up?

Would his presence be overshadowed by his brooding discontent, thus causing a whole cascade of undesirable events that potentially make the evening heavier for everyone?

What do you think?

Dishonoring Your Truth Dishonors Everyone

Personally, I've helped trigger immense amounts of emotional pain in others and created it for myself by not honoring my truth. In most cases, it's because I thought it would be more kind to not share and honor my authentic truth. I have often believed that others are too sensitive, so I couldn't bear hurting them by not giving them what they want, even if what they want is not in alignment with what I want.

Aware now that the world is my mirror, I can see clearly that believing the world around me is deeply sensitive is but a reflection of my own raw sensitivity.

By projecting my sensitivity onto others, I've prolonged relationships that did not feel deeply right to me. I've promised things to people I love because I knew they wanted to hear the promise, even though I had no real desire to deliver on it. Often I didn't deliver. Or I delivered an experience devoid of my enthusiasm, which I find is rarely what anyone genuinely wants from me.

I've been dishonest with requested feedback that might have saved people time, money, embarrassment or aggravation, because I feared they would be too sensitive to hear the truth, which again is just a reflection of my inability to sometimes hear the difficult truth. Not surprisingly, the more I have grown comfortable with receiving painful honesty or criticism from others, the more comfortable I have become at sharing my own difficult truths with others.

Along my journey I've done all those crazy things and more as that fearful voice in my head insists my truth won't be kind. It says, "My truth will hurt them, and then they won't like me, so let's find another way out of this pickle."

It's fascinating to notice that the fear of my truth hurting someone else comes back to the fear of hurting myself. It hurts me to see you hurt, so to spare me the pain of seeing you in pain, I'll just shade the truth a blander tone.

Eventually this goes awry causing more pain and discomfort than if I had confessed the simple truth up front. I might get what I want for a moment – seeing you feel good, me feeling good, you liking me, giving me companionship, sex, opportunity or whatever – but when the real truth pops to the surface like a tri-colored beach ball held under water, you're going to be more upset that I manipulated you under less than honest premises.

In denying others the opportunity to see the truth I'm aware of, I'm denying others the opportunity to meet my reality. I'm denying others the opportunity to learn from what I see. They may not want to see what I see, but who am I to make that decision for them?

How can I know what they're ready for?

How can I know what would serve their highest good? Even when I think I do, can I absolutely know what is best for someone else in this moment?

How can I ultimately even know what would really serve *my* highest good?

You Control Absolutely Nothing

Life is an ongoing game of surprise twists and unpredictable outcomes. We dance in the midst of chaos. There's no more guarantee of surviving beyond tonight's sunset if we tell the full truth than if we lie every minute.

I had an experience in Egypt in 2001 that etched this reality into my consciousness like a red hot cow brand on my bum.

Most of the cars in Egypt are in really bad shape. They look as if 50 years ago, someone pushed each one off the top of a tall building, twice, before hopping in and driving away like Fred Flintstone. The family I was living with at the time had a yellow Subaru that looked even worse than that. If Steven Spielberg made a horror movie about a ghastly dead car come back to life, this would be the one that crawled out of the murky junk yard grave to haunt the nearby village.

One day we were driving down a highway lacing the outskirts of Cairo, probably going at that car's top speed of 50mph. Suddenly, with no warning, the car abruptly veered left and smashed sideways into the metal median barrier, screeching to a violent halt just feet from oncoming highway traffic rushing past the other side of the median. If that barrier hadn't been there, we would have darted into oncoming traffic for an impromptu afterlife rendezvous with the ancient Pharaohs.

As we stood around the car trying to understand what happened, engulfed on all sides by chaotic, choking Cairo traffic, the driver grabbed the steering wheel and spun it round and round like a child's toy. The car's wheels didn't move. The steering wheel had detached from the steering axle. The steering wheel had stopped steering.

I had never heard of such a thing!

How does a steering wheel just suddenly stop steering while speeding down the highway?

This was an unforgettable reminder that we don't control much of anything. I had always taken for granted that I steer my car. I can't control what other drivers do, but barring an ice patch or a seizure, I'm the one who makes my car go in the direction I want it to go. Right?

Turns out that, nope, I don't even control that. I only get the illusion of control, so long as the steering wheel continues to cooperate.

This lesson landed hard and forced me to acknowledge that all my assumptions about having control were just that: assumptions.

I only ever have the illusion of control.

I never know if I'm going to wake up with a tree on top of me, if I'm going to have a kid who lives beyond his first birthday, if the bank is going to steal my money, or if my own body will one day revolt and begin devouring itself via some rare autoimmune disease.

Our own minds and bodies function at the mercy of the mysterious clockwork within. I don't even control the vast majority of my thoughts. While it seems I've developed the ability to scour for the good in all situations, I still can't prevent the perverse from making regular uninvited appearances.

Just today, in southern California, as I'm writing this chapter, a random, unsuspecting young man was pulled out of his BMW at a stop sign and shot dead by another man on a frenzied murderous rampage. The victim was selected completely at random. He could not possibly have known or even suspected that he was eating the last breakfast of his entire life this morning.

We control nothing.

Not our cars. Not other people. Not our partners. Not our bodies. Not our own fates.

Lying and manipulating the truth is one way we fool ourselves into the illusory sense of control. It's our way of pretending we can influence what happens in the very next moment.

Of course we can influence it. We can point the steering wheel in a direction and hope the car goes where we want to go. Usually the car will go that way. We're learning how to build great cars. The crazy thing about real life, though, is that the steering wheel was never connected to the axle in the first place.

Ever heard that joke: Know how to make God laugh? Tell her your plans.

Living anything other than our authentic truth in the midst of this wildly complex universe is quite literally insane.

Kindness is The Way of Things

The truth is always kind because it always honors reality, at least what we can perceive of it.

One can make the argument that illusions are often better than so-called reality. When I was in the military, a female lieutenant confided in me that if her husband ever cheated on her, she would not want to know about it. She would prefer to live the illusion that he hadn't.

Perhaps that situation really is preferable for her, but I would rather have a partner alongside me unburdened by the guilt of inauthentic, deceitful behavior. I would much rather have a partner courageous enough to show up in the fullness of who she really is, rather than be living some secret life she's too ashamed, embarrassed or scared to share with me. Honesty is the foundation of genuine intimacy. I want to experience the intimate world of the one I'm building a life with. It seems infinitely kind to me that my partner share that world with me, even the challenging parts.

I want to live my life as close to truth as possible. This is just another way of saying I want to live the life I, alone, was born to live. It seems insane to merely indulge myself for 100 years in murky ways of thinking that cause me stress and keep me ignorant.

In the case of my lieutenant friend, her desire to stay ignorant is only driven by her desire to avoid the pain that inevitably comes with total disillusionment. This pain avoidance runs rampant in our society, leading us to take massive amounts of pharmaceutical drugs and engage in all varieties of destructive addictive behaviors that only work to numb our physical and emotional pain rather than deal with the root causes of it. As a result, the root causes persist, and we live with the myriad consequences unleashed upon us by our superficial solutions.

Ignorance is bliss only until the hidden truth reveals itself, and it has a knack for doing so at terribly inconvenient moments.

Perhaps you still think reality isn't kind.

Perhaps you think it wasn't kind to the man that was randomly murdered today. Perhaps. Yes, there will be suffering. His loved ones, friends and family, will grieve enormously.

But think also of the countless parents who will hug their children a little longer tonight. Think of the people working unsatisfying jobs who dream of something better, who will be inspired by this random tragedy and figure they better get a move on lest chance come for them next. Think of the gift of gratitude and increased awareness of our fragility that this man's unfortunate demise leaves on the doorsteps of countless human beings tonight.

Even his grieving family and loved ones – if they can find a way to not let this loss simply break their hearts, but break their hearts wider open – they will discover unforeseen new depths of joy and appreciation for this precious life that offers no guarantees and claims us all eventually, one way or another. Then they, too, may discover the enduring kindness of reality.

> *The wound is where the light enters us.*
> *– Rumi*

Through our wounds is often how we truly touch the world and experience ourselves an integral part of the whole of existence. Heartbreak shatters the intellectual armor we encase ourselves in so we may finally feel the visceral, pulsating rhythm of the universe coursing intimately within and all around us.

That's how life finally found me.

It was wrenching heartbreak, found in the despair of an imploding marriage and the persistent failings of later romantic relationships that finally began to rip holes in the full-body condom preventing me from deeply *feeling my life.*

What looks unkind is only salvation in disguise. It's freedom from our false stories, including the biggest lie of them all: that we've got plenty of time on this planet to find happiness.

In his famous Stanford University commencement speech, Steve Jobs emphasized the galvanizing effect of accepting that we are, in fact, going to die:

Remembering that I'll be dead soon is the most important tool I've ever encountered to help me make the big choices in life. Because almost everything – all external expectations, all pride, all fear of embarrassment or failure – these things just fall away in the face of death, leaving only what is truly important. Remembering that you are going to die is the best way I know to avoid the trap of thinking you have something to lose. You are already naked. There is no reason not to follow your heart.

Yes, it is wildly painful when our illusions burst, as when a loved one dies or simply leaves us, but like a crushed flower emanating sweet fragrance under heel, the difficult loss can yield new appreciation for how little time we have to live the dream dancing in the heart of our authentic truth.

In this way, living our authentic truth is absolutely the kindest gift we can ever offer ourselves or another.

The best gift you can ever give another is your own happiness.
– Abraham Hicks

REFLECTION QUESTIONS FOR JOURNALING

Choose at least one question to explore:

1. Can you recall a time when someone told you a painful truth you were not ready for, but that ultimately proved to be a blessing in disguise?

2. If there is some personal truth you are holding back for fear it might hurt someone, can you find three examples of how confessing it might be the kindest thing you could do, for them AND for you?

9

Your Truth Is Only About You

An essential aspect of your authentic truth is just that: it's yours.

Imposing it on other people is like making them think with your brain, feel with your heart, see with your eyes when they have perfectly useful organs to work with themselves (regardless how well you think they're using them).

I'm partially color blind. It is estimated that 10% of the population experiences some variation of color blindness, and there are many variations of color challenges that people may have. When I managed an independent music band, we toured North America in a purple SUV truck. Especially at night, the truck took on this beautiful rich dark purple sheen. It was gorgeous. Except it wasn't purple. So say the band members. I still don't really believe them. But I have a form of color blindness, so I had to take them at their word. Still, what's a color, anyway?

Your authentic truth is like that, too.

Just as my eyes have the capacity for seeing the world a certain way, so too does your truth represent a reality that likely isn't fully true for another person in the same way it is for you. Anyway, who's to say their blue is any better than my purple?

It is essential to understand this funny quirk of human perception, as so much conflict, if not all of it, happens because we don't.

You Alone Decide What Is Your Truth

In Los Angeles' ruthless gang culture, when one member of a gang is shot, that gang's immediate reaction is to retaliate and shoot a member of the rival gang. In October 2005, a student in Watts was wounded in a midday drive-by shooting. Within 4 hours of that shooting, 20 more occurred, one retaliation after another. This is the pattern of war, a cycle which has repeated itself for decades leading to thousands of gang-culture related deaths.

Cynthia Mendenhall, previously known as Sista Soulja, was a high-ranking member in the 1980s of one of the oldest Crips gangs in Watts, CA, in south Los Angeles. The *New York Times* wrote, "Mendenhall grew up amid the economic and social wreckage of working-class Watts. As a young child, she says, she was routinely molested. Her mother started drinking, then using PCP. By the fourth grade she was fighting in school. … At 11, she joined [the PJ Crips gang], eventually winning fame throughout the projects as a fighter – even while pregnant."[1]

Mendenhall came of age in an extremely chaotic culture steeped in cycles of profound frustration, victimhood, rage, aggression – survival of the most violent. She would quickly emerge as one of its most powerful leaders.

In Aug 2006, her son Anthony was shot and killed in a drive by shooting. Three months later, her other son, Darrian shot himself dead during an altercation with police, right before her eyes. However, by this time, Mendenhall had long since abandoned the hopeless culture of gang warfare and turned instead to community and political activism.

Mendenhall's response after both deaths was not to seek retaliation, but instead she issued an impassioned call for healing and reconciliation. She publicly asked all parties not to retaliate, against neither rival gang members nor the police, whom many believed were to blame for Darrian's panicked suicide.

Remarkably, she was able to resist believing her culture's typical thoughts – the very popular thoughts of our entire Western civilization – that insist the only way I can feel better is if someone else suffers massively for what happened to me. I can only imagine that such thoughts must have passed through her mind, and I don't want to make light of her experience. Mendenhall, watching her two sons die within three months

---

1. New York Times article. 2013. http://www.nytimes.com/2013/07/14/magazine/what-does-it-take-to-stop-crips-and-bloods-from-killing-each-other.html?pagewanted=all

of each other, must have experienced an agony beyond comprehension.

Rather than make her sons' deaths mean that someone else must pay with their lives, too, her deeper truth had their deaths mean that something in her community needed profound healing. Her deeper desire for wholeness and harmony formed her response to the situation, rather than the common mind's automatic inclination towards blame and retaliation.

If a mother who grew up immersed in gang culture can watch guns take the lives of her two sons and heed a deeper call within for healing rather than revenge, then any of us can take any situation and heed the deeper wisdom within rather than simply project our unquestioned fury outward.

Nelson Mandela is another powerful example as a man globally admired for forgiving and even embracing the privileged white men who kept him jailed for 27 years. His ability to connect with a far deeper authentic truth, his clear vision to live in a free and equal society for all South Africans, black and white, led him to look past any negative judgments he may have thought about his white jailers.

Instead, he focused on actions he could take to instill a sense of unity among all his countrymen. As President of South Africa, he quickly engaged in controversial actions, like publicly rooting for the country's all-white Rugby team which was perceived by blacks as just another oppressive bastion of white racism. Mandela was operating from a deeper truth living within his own being that had nothing to do with anyone else's behavior. Because of this, his name lives among the greatest leaders of our modern era.

> *They may take our lives, but they will never take our freedom!*
> *– William Wallace (Braveheart, The Movie)*

I am not suggesting other people's destructive behavior should go unaddressed by our society. I am merely suggesting that our own personal truths are not dependent on their behavior. People can do whatever they want, say whatever they want, think whatever they want; our own inner authentic truth remains untouched. It may be stirred up by their actions, but it will not ever be determined by them.

Your truth really has nothing to do with anyone else – not what they say, not what they think, and not even what they do. Yes, other people's actions and words can affect us, in profound and life changing ways. But how we are changed by them depends entirely on the meaning our minds create in response to what we observe. Most of us have no conscious awareness of our thoughts, and we spend our entire lives simply reacting to what happens in the world outside ourselves in fairly predictable ways.

Without the ability to create space between our thoughts and our identity, we're little more than sophisticated meat machines running pre-loaded thought-software. Provided the imagined consequences don't deter us, we act out our thoughts without really questioning them. Too often, we do so to our own detriment and the detriment of those around us.

Our authentic truths, on the other hand, while perhaps arising in our awareness as we witness outside events, are not borne of those outside events. What is authentically true for us in any given moment is not directly a product of events taking place in the outside world, even when those events are murderously violent.

Authentic Truths and Inauthentic Judgments

Our judgments, on the other hand, are completely determined by the outside world. In fact, our judgments are essentially created and instilled in our brains by the external world. They're not even our own. They are but inherited ideas, concepts, biases, traditions, preferences, beliefs, etc. injected into us by our families, communities, and the culture that surrounds us.

Learning to distinguish these unquestioned, inherited judgments from our individual authentic truth is an enormous breakthrough.

We can look to the gay community to see how this phenomenon has clearly played out in the last 30 years. Facing the overwhelming condemnation of the world around them, countless homosexual people chose to stay "in the closet" for years, justifiably terrorized to live openly their authentic truth. Some homosexual people even adopted their communities' condemnation of homosexuality and made it their own, thus creating agonizing internal conflict while living secretly in shame. We still see that today in religious attempts to "cure" homosexuality, with those leading such programs often being people who admittedly experience innate homo-sexual desires.

We routinely adopt the insanities of the world as our own.

As our clarity grows and we start to become aware of the unre-liable judgments and unquestioned thoughts we've merely inherited from the outside world, we start to notice the deeper rhythms stirring more quietly within that would serve as the true compass for our lives.

We begin to see more clearly that our unique, individual truths have nothing to do with anyone else.

The truth becomes intimately personal. We can no longer look at the outside world and make definitive judgments about what we see. This won't stop us from doing so – I still do every day. It does, however, dramatically loosen the psycho-logical stranglehold those judgments put around our necks, which in turn helps break the psychological strangleholds we put around other people's necks.

I still make ugly, negative judgments about the outside world that my mind insists are true. However, this little bit of aware-ness empowers me to acknowledge that they *aren't absolutely true*, and therefore I don't need to force them on anyone else. I no longer need anyone else to believe my judgments, because I no longer fully believe them myself.

BRYAN REEVES

Maybe I do think some guy is a total asshole in this moment. I may be completely justified in saying so; maybe he just insulted my sweet mother. However, it's remarkable to both acknowledge that I'm having this angry thought about another person while simultaneously acknowledging that I don't have to do anything about it or even believe it. Truly, observing my own thoughts can even be hilarious.

I lived with a music band once. Six men living in a tiny 3-bedroom Los Angeles house, after ten months touring North America together in an SUV (it was definitely purple). One would think this a masculine recipe for volatility. Sometimes this was true, but for the most part, not really. We were six men with a high level of awareness that our "stuff" was never about anyone else, so we rarely blamed each other for our own discomfort. Thus, we very rarely fought. When we did, we got through it impressively fast.

One day, Jaime, our guitar-vocalist, and I split a nice bottle of wine a fan had given us after a concert (we had classy fans). None of the other guys had seemed interested, and we'd already had it for months. Alex, one of the three hotheads in the group with a forceful demeanor, noticed the empty bottle in the kitchen and immediately protested. Alex's voice began to assert itself throughout our tiny kitchen dining nook, where a swarm of hungry musicians was scurrying about preparing dinner before American Idol started on the living room TV.

I, one of the other three hotheads in the group, immediately challenged Alex's protest. We quickly descended into a heated

184

back and forth exchange, each one retaliating against the other's last accusation. The argument threatened to explode.

Then, just as *American Idol*'s TV audience thundered applause in the background, my awareness shifted away from defending against Alex's frustrated protests and curiously zeroed in on the angry thoughts coursing through my own head. Suddenly, I became a simple witness to the thoughts I had just been vomiting out of my mouth.

With my attention turned towards the thoughts themselves, rather than anything about Alex, I blurted out, "Look, I'm pissed right now and I know it has nothing to do with you, ok! Yes, your complaint seems to be pissing me off but I know ultimately in the end that can't really be true because you're not responsible for how I feel and so I must somehow be full of shit even though I can't see it right now, and I'm talking in this impassioned, high-pitch crazy man voice because I feel agitated for some reason which intellectually I know has nothing to do with you! I know it's not your fault that I'm getting upset right now … even though my brain thinks it is and I want to tell you to go to hell but I won't, because for whatever reason I'm feeling a bit crazy and I have all these thoughts about the wine and you and the past and right now and … well, it's just a mess up in my head right now and that's all!"

It was like blasting white extinguishing foam on a kitchen fire.

My agitated, rambling confession that I knew I had a big mess happening in my head that Alex was not responsible for put immediate brakes on the argument.

There was nothing for him to defend against anymore, because I stopped making my upset about him.

Alex then also became aware that he was merely reacting to an angry assessment his brain had made about what Jaime and I had done.

Like a racing boat cutting back the throttle, his voice's agitated cadence immediately began to relax. With a sly little smile on his face he said, "Ok, man … fine! I get it. Me too … In my brain I'm thinking I'm upset that you guys drank the wine without asking me but in the end I know my frustration has nothing to do with you and I just need to vent and I'll get over it and it's just my thing and we'll both laugh about this in a minute as soon as we get all the energy of it out!"

And we did laugh about it just moments later.

Being able to identify and openly acknowledge the agitated, angry thoughts we were having – rather than simply acting on them – created enough space in the argument for us both to offer sincere apologies. Me, for not asking Alex if he wanted some wine, and Alex, for getting upset so quickly.

It may seem a small example; it was just a silly bottle of wine, after all. But people regularly create an exhausting amount of stress and damage in relationships because of otherwise minor transgressions like this. In fact, relationships routinely end as the weight of such stress accumulates over time.

In the extreme, we shoot and murder each other because we fail to recognize that we're merely experiencing crazed thoughts at this moment, thoughts we don't actually need to believe or act on.

I am not suggesting we tolerate and accept behavior we don't want in our midst. I do not advocate giving ourselves to abuse or aggression. This is about reclaiming our power to live our lives truly at choice and not as purely reactionary victims and unquestioning robots acting out inherited programs when life shows up in ways we don't understand or agree with.

Accepting that our truth is entirely personal, that it has nothing to do with anyone else, is among the most liberating experiences a human being can ever hope to have. For in that moment, we stop being a victim.

In that moment, we become the empowered creators of our lives.

Owning Your Truth Liberates Everyone

Taking responsibility for our own experience liberates others from the duty. People have a difficult enough time managing their own psychological and emotional state, if they manage it at all. Burdening them with the need to manage our own, too, is just too much for any human to bear.

> *The best gift you can give your partner is your own happiness.*
> *– Abraham Esther-Hicks*

More and more I realize that *my authentic truth* is entirely all about me. If I'm telling emotionally charged stories about who I think you are, what I think you've done, or what I think should happen to you as a result, then I'm not actually speaking my truth. I'm merely vomiting some unquestioned externally focused judgments.

My authentic moment-to-moment truth is not buried inside complicated fantasies or philosophies. It's not a sneaky ploy to get others to do or be something that would scratch my itch at the expense of theirs. It's certainly not an angry thought spat out at others like a grenade designed to blow up their self-image.

My truth in this moment is simply a perfect reflection of all that is genuinely real for me right now.

It might first show up as an angry thought about the world around me, but I've learned not to stop there. I know to dive deeper into anger, that there's a far more compelling core truth around which my angry judgments orbit like cold, icy moons.

Even if I'm experiencing absolute, claw-someone's-eyes-out hatred and disgust for what another said or did, it's still only about me.

I know this may not be easy to accept. These are not popular concepts I'm proposing, and we have an incredibly dysfunctional relationship with the actual world around us and with our own selves. We live in a victim-victimizer culture, a world oriented towards vindictive punishment as a way to maintain stability. We routinely color human beings bad and evil and then imprison them forever, whether in actual jail cells or in mental prisons constructed by our own imaginations. Sometimes we just burn them on the modern electric stake, obliterating any hope of redemption.

When others feel attacked, blamed, or threatened, their natural first reaction is to defend themselves. Refraining from attack and blame, while simultaneously honoring our own truth, can eventually create enough space for a dialogue that can't otherwise happen when one of us is preoccupied with our defense.

When we hate or despise or engage in persistent anger with others, we are drinking poison in the hopes that someone else will get sick [*origin of this metaphor unknown]. Hatred is literally poison to our own bodies. Like anger and resentment, it constricts our blood vessels and floods our bodies with toxic chemicals. Chronic anger, hatred and resentment generally do more to harm ourselves than the external object of our fury.

You Give Everything Its Meaning

You're certainly welcome to continue embracing and focusing your judgments on how others' behaviors should be different. People act in ways that are harmful to others all the time. However, for the sake of this exploration into living in the truth, what's happening on the outside world is less relevant than your internal emotional and psychological state.

If your husband or wife cheats on you, you're completely justified in being angry, even hateful. Actually, you're completely justified feeling whatever you feel! I'm not arguing against feeling what you feel. But your feelings are purely the result of the meaning that you give an experience. Unfortunately, our society is heavily conditioned towards meanings that make us either victim or victimizer.

When something "bad" happens and we feel terrible, we generally accept that we feel terrible because the bad event happened.

We never acknowledge the real reason we feel terrible: *because we made the event mean something terrible.*

We do this individually because we do it collectively, as a culture. In some ways, society is created around agreements on what we identify as "terrible" (we make laws and customs to prevent "terrible") and what we identify as "great" (for which we offer incentives, awards, degrees, applause, approval).

In the case of the cheating husband, friends and family will likely label it "terrible," a disgusting betrayal. However, it just might land in the long-ignored wife's lap like an invitation to the marital freedom she'd been secretly longing for. She might be feeling more relief than anger! She's made the event mean "free at last!" (no doubt with a generous severance package). It's possible she'll act out the anger and upset and betrayal just to stay in alignment with the outside world's expectations. While inside, she's ecstatic.

What happens to us outside is not the determining factor for what happens to us inside.

There are couples who get through infidelity with more kindness than anger. They may not stay together, and it may still hurt deeply, but a keen sensitivity to the weakness of our humanity can allow them to move through the experience with more understanding and care.

If you believe in the basic innocence underlying all humanity's sins, you can bypass hatred straight for love and understanding, even for a cold-blooded murderer.

We respond to events in the outside world in all kinds of ways. But the way we commonly use language reveals our deep belief in victim-victimizer culture: "he made me angry"; "she made me horny"; "that made me sad"; "you make me laugh"; "you made me cry"; "you hurt my feelings."

As a culture, we take virtually no responsibility for our internal experience. We'll even swallow magic pills with bad side-effects before taking responsibility.

Certainly all actions have consequences, both for ourselves and the world around us. There is no question of this. When someone murders another person – and I use this example because it's an incredibly challenging scenario to wrestle with and therefore most useful – clearly not just the deceased person's life is affected, but also the lives of the families and friends of the murdered and the murderer, the police investigating the crime, the judge overseeing the case, the community exposed to the crime, and on and on. Trace the connections far enough and we discover the entire world is affected by one event.

Yet our individual experience of these events is entirely personal.

Life is like a joke that cracks me up while you sit there scratching your head. My laughter is less a product of the joke itself than a reflection of my inner world. You didn't laugh because your inner world isn't configured to produce laughter in the face of that same experience.

Similarly, to the things that offend you others will react in different ways. For an offense that one person will resent for a lifetime, another will merely shrug off and return to contemplating dinner.

What we experience is always entirely personal. It's based solely on what's happening in our inner world: what beliefs we hold, what knowledge we have acquired, what dreams we're nurturing and what nightmares haunt us.

Despite the judgments our thoughts create, no matter how clever and right-seeming they may be, the emotion we experience ultimately has nothing to do with the person we think caused it.

You're not upset for the reason you think."
– A Course In Miracles

This is really an exciting discovery.

We're no longer at the mercy of the outside world to determine our state of being. We get to be happy, sad, angry, glad – and it's never anyone one else's fault. We're perfectly free to choose our response. We get to be ok as much as we want to. When we want to feel upset, we get to feel that, too, and we don't need to demand anyone else suffer for it.

We can take whatever actions feel appropriate in response to the world around us. Only now we have the self-awareness to take more inspired action from a place of our raw, authentic, delicious truth.

Life still happens outside our control. We just no longer experience it as victim.

Which is the very definition of empowered. And free.

REFLECTION QUESTIONS FOR JOURNALING

Choose at least one question to explore:

1. Can you think of an external event that deeply upset you, but that, to your surprise, did not deeply upset someone close to you? Why do you think that happened?

2. Think about someone in your life that routinely upsets you. Can you reframe your upset in a way that does not insist they need to change for you to be happy? (hint: What do you think their presence is trying to teach you about yourself?)

10

The Intellect As Servant To The Truth

> *It is no measure of health to be well adjusted to a pro-*
> *foundly sick society.*
> *– Krishnamurti*

In Western culture, we worship the intellect, thought, the mind. We've cast aside intuition, embodied knowing beyond the reach of rational thought, as a reliable arbiter of truth. Instead we've placed the entire burden of "proof" on what our brains alone can accept. If we can't prove something by having it make sense to our logical thinking, it has no value and can't be "true."

Even religious leaders, despite their marketing which insists they're cut of a different cloth than scientists, have been in the intellectual propaganda game for centuries. Major religions have built centuries-old empires by shaming humanity into denying and distrusting our bodies, particularly the sexual experience where our intellect so easily loses control.

As a result of these ancient, sweeping efforts by the collective ego to disembody humanity and entrap us in its mental prisons, we've grown disconnected from the wisdom embodied in our cells, our flesh and tissue, in our very own hearts.

This disconnect reveals itself physically as we get fatter, sicker, and more dependent on pharmaceutical solutions to address it all. Massive industry is dedicated to creating magic pills that allow us to continue ignoring what our bodies scream at us through sickness and disease. It bewilders me to see national TV commercials proudly proffering stomach acid reflux suppression pills as a way to keep us eating whatever our addictions demand we eat, never mind the warning messages our bodies are practically yelling at us.

Naturally, this disconnect is showing up in our deteriorating earthly environment. How can we honor the wisdom of our earthly body when we don't honor the wisdom of our human bodies?

We have created a culture whose intellect is over stimulated and whose heart is sedated. En masse we prioritize financial and material accumulation over the exploration of what it means to be human. Even psychologists who study the fascinating realm of human behavior haven't historically been considered "real scientists" by the more black-and-white logic-based scientific realms of mathematics and physics.

Truth Doesn't Care What You Think

The truth is ruthless, though it has no personal vendetta against you or any other. The truth just is what it is, and it doesn't care what you or anyone else thinks it should be.

It doesn't seek approval from anyone. Not even you. It patiently exists, indifferent to whether anyone acknowledges it or not.

Elvis Presley once said, through quivering lip and thrusting hips, "Truth is like the sun. You can shut it out for a time, but it ain't goin' away."

It is curious how life masterfully conspires – or perhaps how we masterfully conspire with life – to create circumstances that ultimately force us to confront the truth. We might even make ourselves sick.

Author Deborah King writes in *Truth Heals*, "Truth is a force of such magnitude that it demands to be known one way or another. If buried, the truth will push its way to the surface. Denial or suppression of the truth will manifest as ill health, dysfunctional relationships, or financial problems. The truth does not remain silenced or suppressed comfortably."

Living with our truth silenced eventually makes our lives unbearable.

I knew it wasn't in alignment with my truth to wear a military uniform from the first time I tried one on. I would serve my country for 10 years, and I served honorably. But it felt like I was slowly dying every day I woke up and left for work on a military base. I wasn't sure what else I was supposed to be doing with my life, but I knew it wasn't this. Still, I soldiered on, stoic in my misery.

The truth just is. It makes no apologies. It respects no culture, no authority, no laws, no social politesse, no ancestor, no spouse. It bows down neither to the past nor to the future. It offers no blind allegiance to any ideology or faith. It can embrace tradition, but it is no loyal subject to it.

The simple truth is like a wild western stallion, free and untamable. We can rope it, break its spirit and shackle it to the schemes of a vain ego. But by doing so we condemn our lives to the sad, tepid shallows of our potential, never breaking through to experience the wild splendor of our birthright.

The truth is often unsettling. It may be completely at odds with how we think we should be or how the world should work. Our egos may not want the truth to be true.

Nonetheless, there it is, not giving a damn about what our intellect thinks or the rest of the world has to say about it. Just like there I was, slowly dying in a uniform, living out of alignment with some deep truth I hadn't yet the courage to live by.

Authentic Truth Often Defies Society

It's no surprise that our very human, very real truths are routinely at odds with the world around us. Each new generation inherits a distinct culture from its ancestors that it had no say in. In our culture, lying and denying are ingrained in us from birth. We are encouraged from childhood to warp our lives so they fit cultural and familial agendas we had little, if any, say in constructing.

Cultural rules and beliefs evolve as each new generation

arrives and some resist the ill-fitting ways of previous generations.

Looking through history we can quickly appreciate how profoundly our social mores have evolved. Just follow women's
hemlines through the past few hundred years. Of course, we
can see how far we have yet to go until our collective rules
honor our authentic human reality.

As a young man, I grew up ashamed of my sexuality. I've
always been heterosexual, attracted to women my age. Why
would I be ashamed? Because I got so many messages as a
young boy that my penis was dirty, that sex was shameful and
forbidden, that it was something girls shouldn't give up without resistance.

I constantly tried to hide the most natural thing, the reason
humanity even exists: my sexual attractions to women. A
woman practically had to put her tongue down my throat
before I felt comfortable to let on that I was attracted to her. I
had essentially castrated myself.

Western culture maintains this opposition to our innate sexuality throughout our lives. We pretend that married men
shouldn't feel attracted to other women, and yet most certainly do, constantly. Instead of acknowledging and working
with that energy in thoughtful, honest ways, we deny, hide,
pervert and leak that potent sexual energy through a variety
of unhealthy coping behaviors: porn, TV, drinking, drugging,
lying and quietly suffering through it. Conventional culture
also holds that women shouldn't enjoy and want sex as much

as men, yet most do. Many women have higher sex drives than men. Instead of honoring and working with that reality in thoughtful ways, we shame and guilt women into feeling dirty for their sexual desires.

Culture also says it's not appropriate for people to swear, even going so far as to ban certain words from TV. In my first few weeks of college, I was so sure I wasn't supposed to swear that I made myself do 10 pushups every time I said the word, "fuck." Why? Virtually everyone swears; even children. We obviously enjoy it. According to research, it can even be healthy for us by venting stress. What was I trying to get by ending my swearing? Your approval? God's approval? My own?

Another cultural rule that slowly destroys many lives is the one that makes everyone simply get a job, any job, so they can pay bills and have stuff. Yet so many people are either wholly unsatisfied with their daily work, or at best blasé about it, content that at least it pays bills. They fail to see the sad irony that they've created a lifestyle requiring most of their waking hours spent on things that don't really light them up, which means they're living a life they mostly don't enjoy.

I worked with military and government contractors for five years after college. I saw countless zombie humans going through the motions everyday, making their money, paying their bills and waiting for retirement, or a promotion, or just Friday.

As kids, they didn't once dream of reading 12-inch thick technical manuals all day long under pasty fluorescent lights in drab buildings with few windows. I sure didn't. I was miserable those five years I worked at things I didn't care about. How can people do that for a lifetime?

Here's how: we make up all these crazy social rules that live at odds with our deepest truths. Then we believe the rules. Then we live them.

Fortunately, the younger generations experience present culture's disconnects with fresh eyes and hearts not yet imprisoned in calcified beliefs.

Often inspired by brave souls who had the courage to live in truth before them (e.g. Ghandi, Martin Luther King, Nelson Mandela, etc.), a bold subset of the new generation openly calls for deeper layers of truth to be recognized. If "culture" is infested with inauthentic or oppressive society, the call may be more urgent, more subversive, and it may provoke violence.

Those who wisely resist adopting the oppressive elements of their culture inevitably rebel by adopting new ways of being more in alignment with their truth. Some cultures literally murder them for it (like women who want to be educated or choose who they marry in some countries; and men attracted to men).

Throughout history, we passionately admire the audacious artists who express what we may literally be dying to say but can't say, don't know how to say, or didn't even know we wanted to say! Art is celebrated precisely because it transcends the rational mind. Truly great art reconnects us viscerally to the embodied wisdom that lies beneath our normal perception.

Art hijacks our timid caterpillar thoughts and sends us soaring unconstrained into the mysterious realms of wild, untamed truth.

In oppressive cultures where free-thinking is not only discouraged but punished, art still finds a way to out the truth with colorful whispers and scrambled symbols. Authentic artists, unmoved by society's rules and traditions, are subversive conduits by which the truths society denies are brazenly brought into the light. They are clear crystalline prisms daring enough to stare straight into the sun, grab with bare hands sizzling light beams of undiluted truth, and through their very being, fracture that raw light into infinite patterns of breathing rainbow that infiltrate the cold, calculating world of ego mind with disruptive explosions of spontaneous color and exotic form.

History is riddled with artists who shaped awkward unacknowledged truths into physical form, like the controversial 19th-century French Realist painters who painted scenes of real peasant hardship the political class did not want to confront; and the negro spirituals that black American slaves sang on plantations, in corn fields, "as a way of sharing the hard condition of being a slave."[1]

Each of us has such a seditious artist within. Some have locked

1. negrospirituals.com. http://www.negrospirituals.com/history.htm

her deep inside a tiny, quiet, dormant ventricle in their barely breathing hearts, her limbs chained together, her mouth taped shut. Nonetheless, there she waits, an unbreakable revolutionary thirsty to reveal the feral truths that would upend the false beliefs lording heavy over humanity.

As the war for truth rages in the world outside us, between rebellious artist and cultural watchdog, so it also rages within us. We may have her gagged and bound, but the energy we spend keeping her so slowly drains us of our life force.

It seems an inherently human trait to resist anything that threatens established beliefs. We humans crave stability and certainty despite living in an always shifting, uncertain world.

Your Justifications Are Fictions

One of my favorite scenes in literature takes place in *Siddhartha*, Hermann Hesse's classic tale of the Buddha's journey to awakening.

Early in the story, Siddhartha decides one night to forever leave his father's sumptuous palace the next morning. He yearns to venture into the mysterious world beyond the luxuries of the only home he's ever known and search for the truth of existence. His friend, Govinda, surprised and worried, asks if Siddhartha thinks his father will permit his departure.

Siddhartha looks toward his friend; "arrow-fast" are the words used to describe how quickly he discerns Govinda's fear, his weak, passive countenance. Offering no explanation, Siddhartha simply tells his friend, "O Govinda, let's not waste words. Tomorrow at daybreak I will begin the life of the Samanas. Speak no more of it."

Siddhartha knows he is leaving in the morning and there is nothing more to say.

When I read this passage, I am struck by the clear, unyielding force at Siddhartha's back as he chooses to move in alignment with his personal truth. Siddhartha knows what he must do. There is neither explanation required nor anyone who can convince him otherwise. Further commentary about his decision would offer only cheap comfort food to his friend Govinda and unacceptable excuses to his strict father.

Siddhartha knows not what is coming. He's known only privilege and luxury his entire life. He knows essentially nothing of the world outside his palace gates. But on this night, he knows he must leave. Without the commitment to honor his authentic truth of this moment and take the action he knows he must, there is no story. There is no journey. There is no learning. There is no awakening. There is no Buddha. There is no man living courageously at the edge of his authentic truth. There is only another fat king asleep on his throne.

The desire to belong, to feel connected to an experience larger than ourselves, is innate to humans. Like wildebeests afraid to leave the herd lest we get gobbled up by hyenas, we seek justification for our choices in the form of approval from our peers, parents, society, and even our own logical rationale. In a culture that values conformity, it takes great courage to honor an authentic truth that doesn't conform. Fortunately, most of us are not being hunted by hyenas.

There's nothing wrong with justification. A well thought-out explanation for why you will do what you already know you must can muster the courage, garner the support and convert the doubters you might need to move forward ... even if that explanation rests on fantasy.

We have no answers for the biggest questions, the ones we would have to stand on if we were to ever make complete sense of everything. Why are we here? Where is this whole thing going? Why was I born a white man in the USA with massive opportunity while she was born a black woman in a Bangladeshi brothel? Why is my dad healthy and playing golf at 75 while my friend died of massive cancer at 44?

There are no real answers to "Why?" There are convenient pit-stops of understanding along the way, places to rest our tired intellects searching for complete explanations. But if we follow the questions far enough, we will find ourselves wandering into Rumi's wondrous field "out beyond ideas of right-doing and wrong-doing."

The intellect is a powerful tool for navigating the world. If survival is our only concern, the intellect is as good as any tool we've got. But if the arc of our heart's deepest longing is to live a truly exquisite life, a life of beauty and wonder and magic and thrill, then the intellect can only take us so far by itself.

We must surrender knowing to the vast mystery of living, if truly living is our desire.

Poet Rainer Maria Rilke's epic lines in *Letters to a Young Poet*, captured like an invigorating spring-breeze on paper, instruct us well in the art of surrendered living:

> *Be patient toward all that is unsolved in your heart and try to love the questions themselves like locked rooms and like books that are written in a very foreign tongue. Do not now seek the answers, which cannot be given you because you would not be able to live them. And the point is, to live everything. Live the questions now. Perhaps you will then gradually, without noticing it, live along some distant day into the answer.*

A justification implies a rational reason why something must be the way it is. Perhaps there is. Still, that justification is merely a hedged bet against the possibility we might be wrong. It's comfort food for the intellect.

We make up reasons why we think, feel, want or do something to allow the ego to remain in its comfort zone where it thinks it controls and understands everything in the world.

But when we decide, courageously, to forego this comfort food and step outside our comfort zones, into the mysterious unknown, life takes on fascinating new dimensions.

Embrace the Epic Mystery of Life

Many years ago a spirited woman spoke this life-changing sentence to me: "Bryan, even when you're right, you're wrong."

I had just spent two full days laboring to impress her with my aptitude for elucidating the inner workings of humanity. Although she might have been entertained by my philosophical gymnastics, she was completely unimpressed by my conclusions.

"Even when you're right, you're wrong," she spoke softly while sipping coffee at an Italian cafe overlooking the Pacific Ocean.

Her words spent the next year carving out the insides of my hard-earned philosophies and ideas about the world. As I dove into its mystery, it taught me that even my most elegantly formulated philosophies and rich, sensible explanations for basically anything are but rickety patch-work substitutes for *the real thing*.

In other words, I began to see that all my explanations about life are poor substitutes for life, itself. I could not *feel my life* because I was wearing a full-body condom made of thick, stretchable explanations that kept out the raw, wild experience of being fully alive.

Any genuine philosophy leads to action and from action

back again to wonder, to the enduring fact of mystery.
– Henry Miller

My clever mind-made justifications left no room for wonder and mystery.

If we're trapped in merely thinking about life, we miss it completely. So much of life's vast wonder dances in the spaces between rational thoughts.

Max Planck, the very originator of modern Quantum Theory, cautioned us that we are unlikely to ever solve the mystery of nature because we are part of the very mystery we are trying to solve.

This mysterious life force is always conspiring to overwhelm our frightened, stagnant tendencies. It's constantly threatening to burst through the barriers our egos create, which prevent our evolution and retard life's full expression.

That's why your deepest truth does not concern itself with approval from anyone, not even you. Your truth is life itself moving through you, and life requires no justification. Life just is.

This is the work we're up to: breaking through the constricting beliefs our living ancestors gave us that don't genuinely serve life.

We're here to break the intellect's desperate stranglehold it has established on humanity and realign it in service to the inspired movements of heart and soul energy.

We each have something completely new to say about this experience of being alive. We only need look past the hand-me-down thoughts standing in the way.

The intellect is essential as a tool in service of analyzing and strategizing to get things done. It serves us well when we create businesses, build skyscrapers and send rockets to the stars.

But we've made it our master, and it has enslaved the heart's truth. It doesn't embrace mystery, because it can't. The intellect, by its very nature, is antithetical to mystery. It's constantly running to the safety of an explanation, even when those explanations make us do things that don't feel good, like stay in boring jobs or toxic relationships or escape into addictions.

The truth just is what it is. It will find its expression one way or another. If we don't proactively express it out, it will sit like a giant energetic lump in our bodies, sabotaging our relationships, limiting our joy and taxing our well-being.

That's what was happening to me in the military. That's what was happening to me in my relationship with Valerie.

I believe the great challenge of our age is to live deeper than our justifications, to live in the infinite colors swirling around the black-and-white world our intellect knows and feels safe in.

Life is both infinitely large and infinitely small. There is no seeming end to its layers. Our intellect cannot possibly know everything. There are forces beyond its reach, like the wild things, and this is where the authentic truth lives.

REFLECTION QUESTIONS FOR JOURNALING

Choose at least one question to explore:

1. Is there an area in your life where you feel a truth in your body that your thinking mind doesn't want to acknowledge?

2. What might your life look like if you stopped seeking approval for what you know deep inside to be true for you?

11

I Will Not Lie For You

Truth never damages a cause that is just.
– Mahatma Gandhi

One blue-skied northern Arizona spring day when I was in college, a fraternity brother of mine stood in the sunny quad outside the school cafeteria to address a group of brothers casually gathered like any afternoon. I don't recall his whole speech, but I remember the wide whites of his eyes and his essential message: "I will not lie for you. If you're cheating on your girlfriend, do not expect me to cover for you. In fact, if I know about it, I will tell her you're cheating."

He had recently discovered his girlfriend was cheating on him with a fraternity brother.

His words that day were so resolute, so absolute, spoken with such force they left a mark on my forehead like Harry Potter's lightning bolt. This was a revolutionary idea for me at the time: a man telling his man friends, his closest homeboys, that not only will he NOT help cover up secret philandering, he'll dump any can of naughty beans he finds right in the unsuspecting girlfriend's lap?!

I was confused. I knew the offense committed had been bad. But I took for granted this is what guys do for each other: lie, deny, cover up, and do whatever asked to protect and serve each other's monkey business. After all, we're all on the same monkey team, right?

I also saw in his eyes a passionate determination to stand for the truth, and he was a respected older brother that I and everyone else looked up to. Had such a proclamation come from one of the less admired fellas, I may have written it off as a curious oddity for later study at best, if not more justification for why we don't tell this guy where all the parties are.

I will not lie for you.

I will not enable your deceit, your unfair game, your cowardly selfishness, your incongruence, your wholly preventable self-sabotage.

When we lie for our friends, our loved ones, our colleagues and bosses or whomever, we enable their unhealthy relationship with the truth. We confirm their fear that the truth is a sleeping dragon best left sleeping. We may think we're doing them a favor. Perhaps from a certain perspective we are. Our lie, or even silence in the face of their lie, may enable them to keep a relationship, make the money, win the game, stay out of jail. At least in this moment. But we're empowering their insanity, as well as our own.

However, unlike my aggrieved fraternity brother, I am not a proponent for proactively waging the war of truth in other people's lives. It's not my place to mandate the truth in your life. That's your job. I won't try to force you into a truthful life by calling out your missteps; but don't ask me to lie for you, either.

We're All On The Same Team

When I graduated college, I immediately left Arizona for my first military assignment in Oklahoma, a vast land of extremes where sweltering summer heat can ignite a brush fire and soggy winter cold makes the bones ache. I had been in a relationship for a year with a lovely young woman at my university who had a few years left to go before graduation.

I was young, barely 21 years old, and instinctively knew I wasn't up for marrying my college sweetheart. As an harbinger of a pattern you know by now I would later repeat, I didn't want to stay in relationship with her, but I wasn't ready to let go of her, either.

A few months after my assignment began, I spoke with a close friend on the phone who knew both me and my girlfriend. Since I figured he was by far my friend first, I confessed that I had started pursuing other women. I wasn't ready to tell my girlfriend, as I was just … *exploring*.

I expected my friend to support me on this. He was off on his own military assignment and would never see her, anyway. Instead, I remember very clearly that he patiently, gently, urged me to tell her what was happening. Just like when I heard that bold pledge a few years prior, I was confused: isn't my friend supposed to back me up on this?

His unexpected insistence that I come clean shook me. She was halfway across the country, and everything was otherwise fine. I was only feeling out my new post-college life, not making big decisions.

A few days later, with my friend's advice buzzing uncomfortably inside me, she and I spoke on the phone as we did most days. Suddenly, I surprised even myself by confessing I wanted to start seeing other women. It was like suddenly coughing up tacks.

That confession set into course a series of events that surely changed my life and hers. I don't regret it for one second. It was definitely the right thing to do. Yes it pinched, but the truth gave her the freedom to have a satisfying relationship with another wonderful man at college. It gave me the freedom to explore this new adult life without the dark cloud of deceit drifting ominously overhead.

What I admired about my friend's gentle insistence that I confess to my girlfriend is that it honored her as an equal member of the human family. Rather than consign her to the box of "not on my team," my friend stood for her basic human right to know the truth.

I didn't fully appreciate it at the time, but I'm grateful in retrospect for his gentle insistence. His stand also reassured me, even if subconsciously, that he would be very unlikely to lie to me in the future.

It takes great courage to be a stand for truth with our friends. The expectation that we will lie for friends and family is strong. We subscribe to the "us vs them" paradigm. From a broad enough perspective, everyone is "us."

If someone will lie to another on your behalf, you can be certain that given the right circumstances and motivation, they'll lie to you, too.

With this lightning bolt mark on my forehead, a friend recently asked me to lie for him. He was hanging with me and his ex-girlfriend and he knew his current gal wouldn't be pleased, even though he wasn't going to fool around with his ex.

I felt the empathic bro part of me aching to tell him I would "get his back," but then my body began protesting with slight dis-ease. All I could do was promise him I would not contribute to deceit. I did assure him I wouldn't proactively dump the details of his whereabouts. I also offered to answer her with, "please talk to him about it; it's not my place to discuss," which felt to me an honest response under the circumstances.

If I lie for you, I'm only helping you delay your dive into true intimacy. Intimacy is only possible through vulnerability, which means honesty. If you can't yet be fully honest with your partner, start by being fully honest with yourself.

You can't be genuinely intimate with another if you can't be genuinely intimate with yourself.

You can start by taking complete responsibility for your inability to be fully honest at this moment. Diving into that truth alone, acknowledging it as your current reality, rather than putting all your attention on creating and maintaining the cover up, can yield potent fruit.

I don't know what you'll come up with. As you deepen in intimacy with yourself, embracing your own vulnerability and fears inside the challenge before you, you might find the will, even the enthusiasm, to confess the same to your partner. Or you might choose to acknowledge the situation but withdraw from it until you feel ready to dive in. It's even quite possible you'll make awkward peace with your inability to tell the truth, continue lying and suffering the suffocating consequences while living with the risk of getting caught and that outcome's potentially explosive results.

At the time, the friend who asked me to lie for him was in the midst of a genuine and very common human dilemma. He was engaging in social activity he wanted to pursue for his own simple enjoyment. He wasn't cheating on his girlfriend, but he knew she would angrily disapprove. He'd already been caught lying in the past, and those trust issues had not been fully healed. He was caught in that awkward cycle. It should be no surprise that he would complain to me around this time that he did not feel fully free to be himself in that relationship. He ad always been free, and was still now. But he had crammed himself into an awkward little prison of his own making by not fully surrendering to his own authentic truth from the very beginning of his relationship.

The Riddle of Opposing Desires

This is where our deceitful nature shines best: when we find ourselves in situations of apparently opposing desires and we feel forced to make an impossible choice between experiences we so desperately believe we want. It's a maddening riddle whose answer doesn't just elude us, it appears as if no answer exists.

Genuine transformation comes from immersing oneself into the mystery of this Zen-like riddle: *How do I live the life I want today when I'm stuck between two (or more) desired experiences that refuse to co-exist in my life?*

It's a Zen koan, an arguably impossible question the master offers the student to cleverly trick the mind into ripping itself awake: "What is the sound of one hand clapping?"

The secretly disloyal spouse's koan would be: "How do I live content and true, when life makes my torn heart choose: the one in my home who I love, or you, who I'm sure I love, too?"

Like the riddle I once agonized over regarding the world as my mirror, this riddle is the wardrobe doorway to an exciting new kingdom. A kingdom where total freedom is the reality and having everything you authentically want is the natural order of things. Entry to this kingdom is hard-earned. It's not enough to have intellectual answers to this riddle. You must solve the riddle such that the answer dwells in the entirety of your being, living through you like light through a lamp.

I will not offer the answer to this riddle in this book. I don't have it for you, anyway. You can only resolve it and the challenges it poses for your life by leaning boldly into the question, not stealing your way around it.

Remember Rilke's poetic invitation to live the questions, to live everything, that "you will then gradually, without noticing it, live along some distant day into the answer."

Our humanity is faced with such dilemmas every day. The popular expression, "You can't have your cake and eat it, too," points out that you can either eat your cake, or you can have it in cake form by not actually eating it. But you can't both eat the cake and have it at the same time.

Clearly this is true. It's a basic rule of physics. Much like you can't be human and be a dog at the same time. It's one or the other. Though I know very few people trying to simultaneously be a human and a dog. Zero people actually. But eat their cake and have it, too? I know plenty of those. I'm often one of them.

Thus this riddle regularly taunts us in situations where love, companionship, money, and broader life circumstances are involved. We want to live honestly, but we also want to get rich fast. We want to play by the government's rules, but those rules obviously aren't fair and we don't want to lose our home. We want our stable home partner to keep being there when we come home at night, but we also want that cute new intern at the office.

On the surface, we want Experience A, but the mesmerizing allure of Experience B is so overwhelming that we feel we must have it, too. The spoken rule of the game is simple: pick one.

With no obvious answer dancing in front of our face, we start looking for a way around "pick one." Lying is usually the first magic wand we reach for. We enlist our own cleverness, our friends, technology, whatever tools we have at our disposal to manipulate the rules of the game so we win.

And we win, or so it appears, because it looks like we get to have everything we think we want. We get to have a stable home life with our partner, and we get exciting sexy time with the cute intern. For a moment.

However, all we've really done is bypass the mystery of the riddle and game the game to meet our ego's self-serving desires today. We learn nothing of intimacy, vulnerability, truth. We don't learn to embrace and transform the sadness and confusion and pain lurking within that repeatedly drives us into all kinds of self-sabotaging decisions. Instead, we learn more elaborate methods of deceit that serve only to feed our self-righteous and greedy napoleonic ego … and we now have to expend even more energy just working to maintain the secret advantage we've won.

For if we're caught, like Napoleon, we'll probably be made to forfeit our ill-gained treasures and suffer exile to boot.

When we choose to stand for the truth, such seemingly impossible dilemmas shoot us through the eye of the riddle into the wondrous journey of our lifetime.

Like humble hobbits and wise wizards, we venture into our inner realms where our authentic desires live as the treasure of our truth. Yes, we may have to grapple with giant ego-eating trolls, orcs ready to cut our self-image down with rusty swords and fire-eyed snake dragons coiled and poised to scorch our precious limiting beliefs to ash. But the profound treasures awaiting us upon each improbable victory are worth every nearly-eaten adventure we endure.

Being a stand for truth, whether for yourself or another human being, means being a stand for that magical journey.

By lying for another, we only help them delay discovery of the rich soul treasure that is rightfully theirs.

REFLECTION QUESTIONS FOR JOURNALING

Choose at least one question to explore:

1. Have you ever knowingly lied for another person? Do you think your lie genuinely served their personal evolution over the long run – or perhaps hindered it? How so?

2. Have you ever asked someone to lie for you? What did you gain from it? What do you think you lost from it? If you were eventually caught, what happened? How do you think it might have played out differently had you simply been truthful from the beginning?

12

Vulnerability is Sexy

Owning our story can be hard but not nearly as difficult as spending our lives running from it. Embracing our vulnerabilities is risky but not nearly as dangerous as giving up on love and belonging and joy—the experiences that make us the most vulnerable. Only when we are brave enough to explore the darkness will we discover the infinite power of our light.

– Brené Brown

It's exhilarating to live everyday in the land of authentic truth.

Sometimes it's like holding your hands up on the terrifying downward plunge of a roller-coaster, trusting the track and safety bars will prevent you from being flung off into a painful distance. Yes, on some days it may seem like the ride derails and sends you into perilous free fall – there are no guarantees here – but life can do that even when you don't live in your truth. May as well keep your hands up and enjoy the thrill.

But that's just a metaphor. You're probably not riding actual roller coasters everyday. Most life derailments aren't going to actually kill you; they're probably even setting you up for some new magnificent experience in your life, if you're open to it. That's what I mean by *let the peace fall where it may*.

It's about surrender. It's about allowing yourself to be vulnerable, hands up, heart thumping, as life rushes towards you and truth guides every moment along the way.

Authentic People Are Sexy People

Have you ever had an experience of such profound intimate heart-connection with another person that you felt all lit up inside, glowing like a little radiant star?

Have you ever simply listened with an open heart as someone confessed an awkward, personal truth that they'd been scared to reveal? Did you not fall in love with them even deeper at that moment?

Experiences of intimate connection happen when all stressful worrisome stories about yourself and another fall away and you're left standing in the midst of the unfathomably rich, direct experience of life, exactly as it is happening in the moment. The elaborate stories we believe, the stressful thoughts our brains tell us, they all get swept aside for a time of resplendent clarity, like storm clouds parting to reveal the sun.

Being vulnerable is an act borne of clarity, when we willingly open a direct channel into our deep being and release the floodgates for our authentic truth to pour out in the presence of another.

Being vulnerable means revealing one's true self. Vulnerability is an offering of raw unfiltered truth without attempting to control the external world. The act of being vulnerable is a courageous act. Author and researcher, Brené Brown, writes:

> *Courage is a heart word. The root of the word courage is cor – the Latin word for heart. In one of its earliest forms, the word courage meant 'To speak one's mind by telling all one's heart.' Over time, this definition has changed, and today, we typically associate courage with heroic and brave deeds. But in my opinion, this definition fails to recognize the inner strength and level of commitment required for us to actually speak honestly and openly about who we are and about our experiences – good and bad. Speaking from our hearts is what I think of as 'ordinary courage.'*

Brené – of the now famous video TED talk on vulnerability – has become a compelling cultural emissary for the power of vulnerability to change our lives for the better. She writes and speaks extensively about the mechanics and benefits of creating genuine connections with other people through first acknowledging and then expressing the truths of our own authentic selves.

Until now, though, our culture has generally associated vulnerability with weakness.

Vulnerability Is Not Weakness

Harvard psychologist, Dr. William Pollack, says men in particular are "shame-phobic — frightened to death to show shame and feel shame. They'll go out of their way to deny anything that will bring them shame. It's tied into the codes of masculinity." It's no wonder our culture is so paternalistic and masculine-dominated. For ages we have demonized the distinctly feminine virtue of vulnerability.

According to one of our civilization's most famous and fundamental creation myths, the story of Adam and Eve, shame was designed into the very nature of our humanity. As soon as they ate from the tree of knowledge, Adam and Eve both discovered a deep shame around their being naked, vulnerable. And it was all feminine Eve's fault.

Is it any wonder we have such a difficult time being vulnerable?

Nowhere in our cultural understanding of that biblical creation story – nor anywhere else within our cultural narrative – do we get the message that raw, authentic vulnerability can actually be strength and not weakness. Our immaturely paternalistic culture teaches this directly to young boys, and young girls get the same message.

Charles Blow recently wrote in the *New York Times*, "We teach boys, overtly and implicitly, that sexual potency is a marker of masculinity and that empathy and emotional depth are purviews of a lesser sex. The ways we force boys to adhere to a perilously narrow reading of masculinity become a form of 'oppression all dressed up as awesomeness,' as Lisa Wade, an Occidental College sociology professor, put it."[1]

Naturally, women perceive this message, too. It's everywhere. That confessing one's insecurities, feeling emotions, having empathy – all merely symptoms of weakness. Vulnerability is contemptible, we learn early.

But vulnerability is not weakness. In fact, confessing our truth in this moment makes us physically stronger. It's lying and denying that create legitimate weakness, for lying weakens the body, create stress that floods our veins with toxic chemicals and nervously hastens our heartbeat.

In fact, that's how lie detectors work. While they aren't 100% accurate – simply being wired to a machine with people staring at you in a brightly lit room can be stressful – these machines are significantly more accurate at detecting lies than most people are. For we can do a decent enough job at faking facial expressions that the average person can only guess correctly 50% of the time when we're lying – pure guessing luck. However, something in our subconscious knows when our mouths are telling stories our brains don't agree with. When we're lying our bodies create tangible, measurable stress that lie detectors can measure.

The act of lying exhausts our bodies; we age quicker, sleep

---

1. New York Times article. 2014. http://www.nytimes.com/2014/01/11/opinion/blow-sex-is-not-our-problem.html?_r=0

less, struggle more in our relationships, laugh less … we're just plain healthier when we tell the truth.

Very few people can pull off stressed *and* radiantly sexy at the same time.

Bullshit isn't sexy. You might be able to light a temporary mud hut fire with it, but it smells terrible and drives others away – even bulls don't wallow in its midst. Why do we continue soaking in it while trying to convince ourselves it's just a warm mud bath?

There's nothing inherently wrong with what's happening inside any one of us at any moment. It's what we choose to do with that information and energy that creates consequences. Even those we can't predict. The world is far too complex.

The common practice of deception, whether lying to ourselves or others or simply being unwilling to share our vulnerability, is like a vestigial organ that no longer serves any meaningful purpose. Perhaps long ago it served to protect physically weaker people from stronger ones, just as it can serve babies to ensure they don't die, but now it just leaches toxic stew into our bodies, into humanity.

Even physically beautiful people often look tired and aged when they live inside prisons of inauthenticity. We instinctively act wary of people wearing their stress. We know it doesn't feel good to be around it because it isn't healthy in our body to experience it.

The Catholic practice of Confession, whatever you may think

about God and religion, at least has healthy side-effects. The act of unburdening oneself of guilt and shame has tangible healing effects on the body. We feel lighter, more free, more clear. Happier.

The people we feel most drawn to are people all lit up, vibrant from the inside. We can not be lit up from the inside when we are living in an intellectual prison of our own making.

It's time for us to live fully embodied in awareness of who we truly are. It's time for us to tell the truth.

Now let's talk about how to do exactly that.

REFLECTION QUESTIONS FOR JOURNALING

Choose at least one question to explore:

1. What stories do you believe about vulnerability?

2. Can you remember a time you completely fell in love with someone (platonically or otherwise) when they were sharing an uncomfortable truth in a completely vulnerable, non-attacking way? What did it inspire in you?

3. Recall a time when you were being genuinely vulnerable with another. What did it feel like? How did it affect the relationship?

13

How To Tell The Truth

Alas! We have arrived.

We've explored what authentic truth looks like and what it does not look like.

Now it's time to tell the truth.

Living in the truth is an art-form, an everyday moment-to-moment practice. Our muscles of deceit, fantasy and incongruence are strong. We are well practiced at telling fantastical stories to ourselves and others, no matter how sane we think we are. We are accustomed to seeing the world through dirty lenses given to us by our families, culture, religion.

Learning to live in the truth everyday is a lifetime journey, one that few ever master and that many never even choose to explore.

My father used to tell me, "All are chosen, but few choose."

You, having come this far, clearly choose to live an inspired life in alignment with your deepest truth.

Reflections on Truth in My Own Life

Before I get to my patent-pending formula for telling the truth, I'd like to briefly reflect one last time on my own life. There are countless moments where I was aware of a deep authentic truth I wish I would have confessed sooner than I did, if I ever did at all. Had I been more courageous in living my truth at these times, my life would look dramatically different than it does today.

I have no idea what that actually means. I have the life I have. I have a good life, and I'm proud of the man I am ever becoming.

I don't believe in regret, for every so-called mistake is an opportunity to learn something profound. Viktor Frankl proposed something I believe worth considering: "Live as if you were living already for the second time and as if you had acted the first time as wrongly as you are about to act now!"

Unfortunately, we don't get to live that second time.

With reflection, however, we can transform into mountains of gold our past experiences that we only thought were big mounds of smelly kaka. Through reflection, we can mine those mountains of gold for all the courage they contain to help us live our truth today. For we can see clearly what happened when we didn't: we spent way too much precious time living dissatisfied and unfulfilled, mere shadows of our massive human potential.

I can't help but wonder what relationships I did not experience because I lacked the courage to honor my own truth. What children were not born? What thrilling adventures did I not go on?

How many countless moments of exquisite beauty and magic did I not give myself (or others) because I did not express my truth at critical moments in my life?

Throughout this book, I've shared stories where I pretended, manipulated, deluded and outright lied my way around uncomfortable confrontations with my own authentic truth.

What would life have looked like had I made the choice to tell the truth and let the peace fall where it may?

I knew within months of joining Air Force ROTC in college that the military was not a good fit for my soul. I was so attached to the easy path it was offering me – college scholarship, money, prestige – that I wasn't willing to face the deep discomfort I was creating for myself by walking that path.

That discomfort ate away at my passion for 10 years until all that was left inside me was an indifference like death. It would take me years to find my laughter again, to rediscover my passion for living. If I had simply honored my truth early on, I would have declined my scholarship as a college freshman and simply found another way to get through school.

When I was backpacking across the globe after the military, I wish I would have told the girlfriend I was dragging behind me that I knew I wasn't going to build a life with her.

As painful as it might have been to lose her affection, confessing my truth would have freed us both up sooner to pursue the lives our hearts were yearning for. I would have stayed in Australia longer, traveling across the entire continent instead of turning around halfway to go back to her for a hug. I would have said yes to a woman's invitation to Thailand when I was stuck in the Bombay airport for five days. I would have sooner forged a path of authenticity for myself rather than continue walking the path of fear and desperate grasping, the path of running *away* from my dragons rather than courageously into the inevitable battle with them.

Just before I married the French woman, my inner voice quietly insisted, "Don't do this." But I did it. I sent myself on an 8-month journey into a living hell. That choice to ignore my inner wisdom took me off the path towards studying International Peace and Conflict Resolution at American University, and as a result there's no peace in the Middle East today (ok, that may not be realistic, but now we'll never know!). The day after we got married in Miami, FL, we started fighting in the car on the way to the airport. She looked at me cold and threatened to undo the marriage. I already knew marrying her didn't feel right. But I wrangled her back from the brink of instant divorce when I could have acknowledged my truth, calmly agreed and saved myself from that impending catastrophe hurtling towards my world like an asteroid.

I wish I would have allowed myself to be vulnerable with Valerie, my new lover, and tell her of my confusion over whether to see my previous lover in Switzerland. Valerie might have run away, but then why would I even want a partner who would run away from my vulnerability?

Instead, I took that secret down a treacherous path on which I would confront the meanest, darkest aspects of myself, and of Valerie, too. Perhaps I'm a better, wiser man for it now ... but what if I had the courage to tell that simple little truth when it arose in me? Would she and I have a family now? Or would the four years I *wouldn't* have spent with Valerie have created the space to love another woman?

It must be said that I was probably not even capable of making different choices in each of these situations. When faced with the choice to acknowledge my truth or not, I was far more practiced at denying it.

I believe we all do the best we can with the information and wisdom we have at any given moment.

Still, if we are to move forward in our evolution and create a more peaceful, loving and thoughtful planet, learning to live authentically in our truth is a journey we must undertake.

Let's do this.

This Is How You Tell The Truth

There are only two reasons we won't fully confess the truth:

1. To get an outcome we think we want
2. To control people's perceptions about us

Since #2 is really about getting an outcome we think we want, there's really only one reason we don't confess the truth: **to get what we think we want.**

That's it. There's no other reason. So often the outcome we see in our mind's eye, the outcome we *think* we want, is actually *not* the outcome that would lead to our greater good and the greater good of the world around us. After all, life has a way of creating fascinating consequences our human brains could hardly dream of.

This is how magic happens in life, all the seeming miracles that bring amazing experiences, circumstances, results and people that you could never have imagined possible.

This happens when you let go of stressful attachments to specific outcomes and other people's opinions. With no reason to distort it, you are finally free to fully live your truth, trusting in life to handle the rest.

Fortunately, living your truth is simple. It's only your cover-ups that get complicated.

Recall this passage from earlier:

> *More and more I'm discovering the crazy truth, that the simple truth is just that: crazy simple. My authentic truth,*

> *like a great business idea, can typically be written down on one side of a small cocktail napkin: I want this. I don't want that. I feel this. I think that. I like this. That hurts. That angers me. Yes to that. No to this. That pleases me. I'm confused. I just don't know.*

With that in mind, here's my patent-pending 3-step process for telling the truth:

1. Breathe
2. Tell the Truth
3. Repeat

That's it.

STEP 1: Breathe

Just breathe, whether that breath lasts 30 seconds or 30 days. This allows you to reflect on whether you're moving from your truth in this moment, or merely playing out a fantasy, some ill-conceived judgment or someone else's belief and not truly your own.

I know for some this is right away a rough start to telling the truth. I'm part Puerto Rican, which probably isn't relevant, but I do have a passionate hot head! I can literally feel heat flash out from my core to my skin when I'm triggered by an outside event that dares challenge my ego!

Sometimes it's all I can do to breathe! But if I want to break-through old programming and not let my agitated "inner ass-hole" gremlin run my world, then learn to breathe I must!

It's a practice. I'm far more practiced at unconsciously react-ing. Living powerfully in my authentic truth is a deliberate practice of thoughtfully, consciously, effectively responding to the world around me and all its wound-poking triggers.

Are you ready to live exquisitely? Connected to your deepest authentic core truths? A living force in the world for beauty, grace, kindness, love?

Then learn to breathe. Before you react.

This will help you separate authentic truth from intellectual fantasy. If you're anything like me, you're far more practiced at blurring the two into one convoluted mess.

Recall from earlier chapters these hallmarks of your core truth in any moment:

- **It's as simple as this sentence.**
- **It isn't loyal to any story, ideology, belief system, cultural rule.** It isn't even loyal to 30 seconds ago. It can change in the midst of everything you think you know.
- **It's unique to you.** It speaks to your experience and yours alone. Only you have the most complete view of all you've ever lived up to this moment, all of which flavors your internal world just so. No one outside you can tell you about your experience.

- **It doesn't concern itself with stressful stories about other people or the outside world.** Yes, what's happening inside you in any given moment is happening in relationship to the outside world. But remember, two different people in the same exact situation may think and react in completely different ways. Your truth is focused on what is real for you. It isn't trying to persuade anyone else that this person or that circumstance is a particular way. Your truth is all yours, and it loves and respects the world around you – even as you might be passionately working to change that world.
- **It is what it is, even if it defies "reasonable logic."** It doesn't need permission to exist.
- **It never seeks to hurt or manipulate another person.** It may be uncomfortable for you and others to hear. It may drive actions and consequences that are painful to bear. It might even have you hurt people in legitimate self-defense. But your authentic truth has no inherent drive to proactively harm or take advantage of anyone.

This moment of reflection gives you space to discern whether you're about to speak your genuine truth or just vomit more intellectual insanity into the world.

It's like allowing all the flittering flakes in a snow-globe to settle gently to the bottom so you can clearly see what scene they're obscuring. Your stories, thoughts and judgments are the obscuring flakes; your truth is the scene they conceal.

STEP 2: Tell The Truth

Speak. Move. Act. Dance. Create. Leap. Live. Love.

Follow the rhythms. Where does life want to lead you in this moment? What does life want to express through you? Telling your authentic truth, whether with your mouth or your body is essentially effortless – you just surrender.

Breathing allows you to connect with your clarity.

Now you simply act on that clarity. Even if that means doing nothing.

There is popular advice about creating the right moment, waiting for the right setting and accounting for other considerations when it comes to revealing awkward truths.

That may have its uses, and your intellect can be a useful tool in designing such a strategy. But beware. That belief is an opening to play small and keep hiding.

You're welcome to keep hiding. You're guaranteed no medals or glory or cash rewards for confessing, walking, and speaking your authentic truth. You might even get ostracized, left, dismissed, ignored, refused, derided and more in this victim-victimizer blame-throwing culture.

But what world do you want to live in?

Do you want to live in a world in which we continue to hide the magnificent, wildly miraculous beings we truly are for fear of being cast out of a fat, lazy herd that wiles away its days running from imaginary shadows in the bush 'till death inevitably claims them, anyway?

Or do you want to live in a world that celebrates our wild diverse humanity? A world in which you are celebrated for the unique child of the cosmos that you came here to be?

If you want to live in that world, then you must celebrate yourself. You must journey into the heart of your deepest authentic truth, and live from that delicious clarity.

Living connected to your clarity is reward enough in itself.

If that means leaving a relationship, leave. Maybe you come back tomorrow. Who knows? Or maybe you stay because your heart, your soul, knows you need to keep burning in the fire of *wanting to leave*, because that's only your false self wanting to run away from your dragons. Remember, intimate relationships is where the false self often goes to die.

When you breathe, reflect and get clear, if leaving is truth to your core, you'll see that you're choosing to leave the relationship because you have a new vision for your life, you want to experience it, and you don't believe you can create that world with your current partner. You're ready to leave the palace, Siddhartha ... and let us speak of it no more.

I witnessed the most beautiful break-up of a couple I was coaching when the wife reached a moment of perfect clarity during one session. She realized she was married to an incredibly good man who loved her, and whom she loved. Yet in this moment, she was finally seized by the clarity she had been denying for months, that life was calling her to other adventures without this good man. His love was so exquisite for her, his respect for her truth so complete, that with sad, loving eyes he accepted her choice, and that was that. It was the most beautiful break-up.

In that moment, they were both free. Free to tell the truth. Free to live it fully. Free to love each other – and love themselves – completely.

In a relationship, you have the precious opportunity to honor your truth without blaming the other person's apparent character flaws for your choices. In other words, you can leave in love, respecting their right to be however they want to be in the world, without smearing your judgmental kaka all over them as you walk out the door.

You can express your authentic experience without ever making other people's faults responsible for it. Often, what doesn't work for you will work delightfully for another.

> *When a thousand people look at the moon, there isn't just one moon, but a thousand moons.*
> *– Krishnamurti (attributed)*

Living in our authentic truth is what life intended for us.

When we live disconnected, we live in perpetual dis-*ease*. We live in disharmony with our true nature.

In the last chapter we explored how vulnerability draws people together. When someone shares from a place of such raw truth that you can see the pain in their expression of it, we fall in love with their heart because that's what is being revealed.

When people express their raw truth, even passionately, without attacking the world or blaming others for their experience, we're compelled to listen.

When we don't feel threatened by their expression we can discover how remarkably similar we all are. We discover how we all share the same thoughts, emotions, fears, insecurities, hopes and desires.

Then something truly magical can happen, even in the most awkward situations.

Through our vulnerable expression of the truth, love emerges effortlessly. Not the conditional kind of love that requires people to do specific things or for circumstances to be a particular way, but the unconditional kind of love that arises regardless what the world looks like now.

It takes courage to tell the truth, but only when we're attached to a particular outcome.

When we set ourselves free to live in our authentic truths in every moment and give the world around us permission to do the same, unconditional love is the natural consequence.

The peace of mind, connection, joy, passion, deep laughter and exquisite love we ache for come to us naturally, almost effortlessly, when we surrender to living our authentic truth and let life take care of everything else. After all, life gave us babies and dogs and watermelon. Life knows what it's doing!

The Feel Of Authentic Truth

I recently had an opportunity to speak an awkward truth when a long-time friend of mine suddenly announced he was in Los Angeles and insisted on staying at my home. I noticed my body tighten at the mere thought of it.

I had plenty of reasons why this was not a good idea, and some of those reasons were related to my thoughts about his character. He's an adopted brother of sorts, and a good person. But I believed if he stayed in my tiny beachside apartment that he would ask me constantly to entertain him or I would feel obligated to. I feared I might be giving myself to babysitting a grown man for four days when I am deeply called to focus on writing and other creative work.

As I breathed into this challenge in between phone calls, I was able to see the many stories I was telling about him based on our past interactions. I haven't seen him in a year, but I already "knew" in my imagination what having him here would be like. I was also able to experience my simple, clear truth, which revealed itself in tightness throughout my body, that taking him in wasn't the best decision for me at this moment, independent of those stories. I realized that if I took him in, the risk was high that I would turn my attention away from writing and towards him, that I would resent doing so, and that he would quickly experience my resentment.

Everybody loses.

I knew that if I ignored my truth and took him in, anyway – which I've done countless times before in countless situations – life would surely present me new opportunities to tell the truth during his visit. For example, I could have clearly communicated that I'm focusing on my creative work and am not, therefore, available to entertain him. Of course, I could not know in advance whether he would respect that. My apartment is small and consistent interaction that took me away from my focus was likely inevitable.

I can't know for sure how it would have gone. I only know the thought of it made me feel heavy.

Before I called him back, I took a deep breath. I clearly saw how telling him "no" was the kindest choice for everyone. So I took another breath, dialed the phone, and told him, "No, the timing isn't good for me to host you."

This happened so recently that I'm writing this paragraph when he would otherwise have been here. This paragraph only exists because I took a moment to breathe, reflect and then speak my simple, if awkward truth, with no drama, no convoluted stories to defend and no arrogant judgments about his character to later regret and apologize for. There might be hurt feelings on his part, but this was an opportunity for his growth as a thoughtful, aware, loving human being, as much as it was mine. Surprisingly, in the last 24 hours I've seen him post gorgeous sunset pictures on Facebook from the beautiful mountain home he ended up at, simply because I honored my truth and said "No, this isn't right for me right now."

Everybody wins.

It was simple as that. Depending on your constitution, that may seem a really tame example to you, or you may understand viscerally my discomfort. Regardless, this example is about my experience with telling the truth. You have your own edge, wherever that may be.

I've learned more and more to connect with the wisdom in my body. By checking in with how my body is feeling at any moment, I'm learning to balance my intellectual justifications with a deeper wisdom that speaks through my body.

The path of truth and authenticity always feels more expansive in my body. It feels lighter, even when it's scary. Living the truth isn't always easy. In fact, it often isn't easy. It may require me to do things that offend my thirst for short-term results and instant gratification. It might have me do things that don't make intellectual sense. An opportunity might look good on paper, but when I think about it I feel like someone just unplugged the electricity from my body.

My French ex-wife looked great on paper. Attractive. Brilliant. French. Doctor. Loves dogs. Wanted me. But in her presence

I routinely felt confused, disoriented, helpless, like in a dream where the faster I ran, the slower my legs moved.

That's one way I have learned to distinguish what my authentic truth is in any given moment. A "yes" to a path, an idea, an experience, a situation, a person, etc. creates an experience in my body that feels expansive, and either positively exciting or calmly reassuring. I might still be frightened by the choice I feel called to make, but that's my intellect telling me ghost stories. That fear might also just be my shallow ego afraid of the lessons my soul wants to learn.

That authentic "yes" can be a call for me to evolve beyond my comfort zone. Evolution requires that something give way, die, so a fresh new iteration of life can emerge.

If the caterpillar thought the cocoon only meant death; she'd avoid it any way she could, same as she works to avoid any other predator. But her butterfly spirit calls her into the cocoon where her body soon turns to mush. The caterpillar dies so the exquisite butterfly can emerge. We humans are no different (except for the silk cocoon part).

Acting from inauthenticity on the other hand feels heavy and lethargic, unexciting and dreadful. It forces me to wear a mask of falsity so the people or circumstances I'm trying to manipulate don't catch onto the game I'm playing.

When I feel a "no" in my body, constriction, heaviness, I go into reflection. What am I choosing that is creating this heaviness in me, and more importantly, why am I choosing it?

I can usually trace my choice to some deep desire or unmet need that I want the world around me to fulfill immediately, at whatever cost. There's nothing wrong with desire or need, and it may be the healthiest thing for me to fulfill that need. When I feel a "no" in my body, however, I'm probably choosing a way to fulfill that need that actually won't.

With this awareness I'm empowered to make choices that support my authentic truth. I can reflect on which choice is the path of expansion and lightness in my body, my authentic "yes," and begin moving in that direction. Or, like my mom said, I can honor my doubt and do nothing but be patient. I can rest assured that life is cooking up something juicy that will meet me in my authenticity. I can never enjoy a juicy authentic meal as long when I'm living incongruent with authenticity.

Here's a few examples of how this occurs in my life today:

1. **I don't do work that doesn't excite me.** I have been offered prestigious gigs in the entertainment industry that a few years ago I would have jumped at. Now, if I can't get excited about it, I don't take the job. You can't pay me enough to spend my time being unhappy. While it ain't fun being broke, either, there are so many ways to make a living that are in alignment with my enthusiasm.

2. **I don't try too hard to convince people of anything anymore.** Every argument I've ever had was an attempt to get someone else to think like me, to validate either my fantasy or my truth – especially in intimate relationships. In the past,

if I could get a woman to respect my truth, it would mean my truth was valid. It would also mean I was worthy of her love. I no longer need anyone's approval for my truth. I also know I'm worthy of love. I do my best to stay open to my truth evolving. That happens as we collect new information and learn new things. I also respect that your truth is as real for you as mine is for me. So I get in less arguments. I don't have as many fantasies to defend, and my truth doesn't need anyone's approval to exist. It's wildly liberating.

3. I don't spend time with people I don't feel good around. When I routinely feel heaviness in someone's presence, I just don't spend time with them. As a relationship coach and life coach, I don't accept clients with whom I don't enjoy working. When I feel drawn to someone I feel heavy around, I know there must be some fantasy story disconnected from reality I'm telling myself that has me stay in their presence. Or their presence is triggering an unhealed wound of mine that my heart is ready to heal. So I do my best to reflect on those possibilities, knowing this is an opportunity to learn something about myself. I try not to focus on how messed up I think this other person is. I wouldn't be drawn to them if they weren't.

4. I don't give myself to inauthentic relationships with women. Sharon Stone said once after a break up, "Women can fake orgasms. Men can fake entire relationships." Sure, men can do that when we live inside our intellectually fabricated stories. As I have learned to live more connected to my authentic truth in every moment, I'm able to be fully authentic with women around what's actually happening for me. I no longer use ambiguity or deception to lull women into short-lived relationships I already know aren't going anywhere. Instead, I'm more able to just confess my deepest truth in any moment. My relationships with women are richer and more rewarding. We may consciously decide not to have sex because our individual truths don't align in this moment. Or we may consciously decide to have sex because in this moment they do. Our intimacy runs deep either way.

Breathe, Speak ... Live Your Truth

It's fascinating how often I still get asked after a lengthy discussion on all this, "So how do you actually do it, though? How do you live/tell the truth when your body seems to practically be screaming that you're going to die if you do so?"

Here's how:

1. You breathe.
2. You reflect.

The stressful story you're telling yourself that's causing your discomfort probably isn't true. Even if it is, are the likely consequences really as dire as you think? What is the likely cost of not honoring your truth? What brilliant life could you potentially be giving up by remaining silent with your words or your actions? Perhaps you need to experience even more pain by deepening in disconnection before you find the courage to come home to yourself. You decide when you've hit the bottom and you're ready to shift your experience. For some people, 10 minutes is too long to live painfully out of alignment with a deep truth. For others, 10 years is too little.

3. You speak.

Say it out loud. To yourself first, if necessary. Practice in the mirror. Then tell someone else. Someone safe, if need be. Then tell the person who needs to hear it. That person may still just be you. But speak it out loud. Claim your truth for yourself. Declare yourself free to give your greatest gifts to the world and live your unique brilliance as we've discussed throughout this book. If you must take action to make things right in the world because you've been dishonest or living incongruently, out of alignment with your heart and soul, then do so.

4. You live.

Live in the direction of your deepest truth, your highest excitement. Take the next step that speaks from your deepest wisdom. It might feel like a whisper in your bones, pulling you in this direction. "This way, this way," it speaks quietly. Follow that little white rabbit. It's bringing you home. To yourself.

We are each on an extraordinary journey of self-discovery.

This journey is messy.

We can forgive ourselves for all the times we have lived out of alignment with our own authentic truth. Contrast is an exceptional teacher. The pain of living out of alignment is often what serves to bring us back home to our true selves.

As we learn to move through our lives as embodied expressions of our heart's deepest truth, we begin to experience a world of exquisite beauty. This world has always been available to us. Only our fear and our grasping – our desperate attempts to reclaim the love that has always been our birthright – has kept us perpetually separated from this blissful heaven on earth, a heaven we have always been immersed in. Like fish who can't see the water, we only need open our authentic eyes to experience the never-ending miracle of this moment.

Living authentically inevitably creates the passion, fulfillment and love you seek. It isn't always an easy path. But then, living inauthentically inside of fantasies that crush your spirit is no gentle uphill slope, either. The choice is yours. Every day. Every moment.

Living your truth is what you came to this planet to do. Life will take care of the rest, as *peace magically falls where it may.*

REFLECTION QUESTIONS FOR JOURNALING

Explore both:

1. What area in your life would be most dramatically affected by coming clean? What are you afraid you'll lose by telling the truth? What is the cost of remaining silent / taking no action?

2. Can you even imagine what you might gain if you told the truth?

Epilogue - You Are Conscious Stardust

> *The privilege of a lifetime is being who you are.*
> *– Joseph Campbell*

Do you know who you *really* are?

Your ancestors are the stars.

You are, quite literally, conscious stardust.

Countless vast millennia ago, deep inside the farthest reaches of cosmic history, our ancestors were forged in the fiery factories of material potential. The heavens were an exploding, swirling hot, electric turbulent soup impregnated with elemental materials like hydrogen, helium, nitrogen, carbon, iron. Our forebears, the stars, were born in this cosmic nursery as primordial material began to clump together, sparking off brilliant burning lifetimes that lasted hundreds of millions of years.

As an ancestor star's lifetime began to fade after eons of resplendent bloom, in one final act of glorious being it would explode with an epic, massive fireworks and shoot its remains outwards on a fiery wind. This liberated primordial material rocketed through space until it found other raw material and reformed itself once again into a completely new star creation.

This cycle continued across the Universe for billions of years as the elements danced excitedly between incarnations of blazing solitary union and explosive surrender to separation and transformation.

Our later ancestors, the planets, would eventually coalesce out of displaced stardust remnants swirling around newly burning stars. This raw material, mostly metals and gases, once itself part of a million other exploding stars, by circumstance and physics now became strong, solid ground upon which other miraculous adventures could unfold.

These newly birthed ideas of stable, sturdy physical structure – planets – would support the emergence of new stardust off-spring.

Planet Earth itself was shaped in the heavens by a cloud of cooling stardust particles twirling endlessly about itself like a massive whirling dervish under the watchful light of its great mother star, our Sun. As this stardust danced its dervish dance, the ancient laws of attraction drew the bits and pieces ever closer together until our planetary home solidified and was born, luxuriating in her mother star's bright, warm caress.

With Earth, as with possibly countless planets like her, the Universe had succeeded in creating an expansive, solid canvas upon which it could now animate entirely new physical forms with its primordial play-doh. Over endless eons of time, as these raw elements continued to be squished and smashed, burned and electrified, drowned and shaken, "Life" began slowly to emerge from the fuss.

Only it didn't call itself "Life" yet.

When it first appeared, what we humans now call "Life" was simply the next movement in the unfolding story of the Universe. Just as stars formed first from the basic cosmic elements and gave way to planets and galaxies, planets were now paying it forward by giving way to a new physical arrangement of cosmic creation dust.

As this new creation of universal imagination evolved, it was animated and guided by the natural laws of cause and effect, attraction (gravity, electromagnetism, chemistry, etc.), energy (electric charge, mass, etc.) and other fundamental principles of physics.

It slowly developed the ability to make sense of its surrounding environment in ever more compelling and far reaching ways. It designed clever mechanisms to hear vibration passing through atmosphere, smell gaseous molecules floating by, feel and even taste other particles nearby. It developed a brain to process this fascinating information. Eventually it would open billions of eyes capable of grasping the infinite array of light photon waveforms that drench the Universe with dazzling arrays of color and visual form.

To explore the world around it and play its role in the universal cycle of life-death-life, this newborn child of the Universe developed all varieties of locomotion, from fins and squiggly tails to long legs and feathered wings. This new "idea" grew more and more able to make sense of the world around it, peering ever farther beyond its immediate surroundings for more information in the hopes of better understanding its place in the world.

One day it began looking curiously towards the heavens, towards the stars, and imagination was born. This new creation began to wonder.

As this new life-form – *this particular formation of Life* – grew in intelligence, imagination and self-awareness, it learned to see itself from outside itself. With the ability to notice its own existence relative to an "other," it invented a concept called "separate" and it finally gave itself a name: "Life."

Thus did "Life" decide it was made of separate parts isolated from each other.

Until this moment, Life had never given itself names that implied separation from any so-called "other." Planets never named themselves "planets." Stars never named themselves "stars."

No, Life only named itself once humans emerged and started staring down at our navels and up at the heavens, fancying ourselves as somehow unique and separate from the rest of the Universe's creation.

This word "Life" which we humans hold so sacred is a fiction made up by our self-consciousness. The distinction of "Life" versus "non-Life" never existed until our clever brains created it. There is simply one Universe, made throughout from the same basic elements, and we are but one of an infinite variety of arrangements of those elements.

There is otherwise no "Life" separate from the planet whose oxygen it breathes or whose food it consumes. Similarly, there is no "Life" on earth, or even earth itself, separate from the innumerable stars in our skies whose very existence ultimately gave way to this planetary canvas.

First, we were stars. Then we became planets as the elements that didn't make it into coalescing stars cooled, gathered and condensed tightly into giant orbs that stayed close to their mother. Today, we are a two-legged form of Life walking about one of these planets after emerging from its oceans and mountains.

The famous Gaia Theory developed by James Lovelock holds that organisms do not exist independent of their environment, but rather co-evolve with it. The Earth's atmosphere and everything on its surface – trees, oceans, oxygen, humans, mountains, termites, clouds – are not simply separate things on the surface of a giant rock called Earth. Rather, all these surface elements are like the skin on a cat, evolved into existence as an intrinsic part of Earth's own evolution.

As our bodies are fed and sustained by the ever-evolving stardust soil and water of this planet, it is a complete falsity to believe we are in any way separate from it.

We are, indeed, Conscious Stardust ... we are Earth, itself, come alive.

We are the tangible manifestation of what was once just a dream of the cosmos to create a universe teeming with self-aware arrangements of its molecules – beings that could say, "I Am" and have a visceral, profound appreciation of what that suggests.

We must be the cosmos' dream because we are here. As the great oak tree emerges from the tiny acorn only by way of an idea encoded in a DNA blueprint, humanity could have emerged from a chaotic primordial soup only if somewhere already encoded within that soup was the actual blueprint dream of humanity.

Now we are here. Stars exploded into Stardust transformed into Earth ... come Alive.

How, in all creation, did we ever decide we must be inherently flawed creatures?

It's nothing short of miraculous that we're even here to ponder such questions.

For as the acorn becomes the oak tree only in the proper conditions, so too did humanity emerge by grace of the precisely proper conditions finally arranging themselves after billions of years.

Are you even remotely aware of the precise mathematics life requires to exist?

If certain universal mathematical truths like gravitational constants were different than they are by even a very tiny bit, life as we define it could not exist anywhere in the whole universe.

Even more, beyond the sheer immensity of the universe itself, each tiny little one of us human beings exists by absolutely, completely, undeniably miraculous conception. The odds we had to beat to come into existence are simply beyond comprehension.

Do you know how many other wildly ambitious sperm you competed against for one lone prize? Something like … zabillions! Do you understand the odds against your success? You can't possibly, because our human minds have not evolved to comprehend numbers like zabillions. We've never directly experienced a zabillion of anything.

You've actually won the most statistically impossible-to-win and insanely-stupid-to-spend-any-money-on Powerball Lottery in the entire known Universe!

I recently heard an economist describe betting on the lottery like betting that one citizen picked at random from the entire United States population will be actor Brad Pitt. In the case of you being lucky enough to be born, imagine your parents picking a random person from 100 Planet Earths … and you're married to Angelina Jolie!

Given the vast conspiracy the heavens have waged to bring each and every one of us to this planet for just a brief

moment, how can we for one moment think our own unique truths are somehow wrong or inappropriate?

Even more, how can we be so ungrateful and thoughtless (ironically) as to not express life's unique truths through these lives we were gifted?

Author Marianne Williamson told us, "Our deepest fear is not that we are inadequate. Our deepest fear is that we are powerful beyond measure. It is our light, not our darkness that most frightens us."

The same forces that created massive pinwheel galaxies, snowstorms, immense salty oceans, dandelions, platypuses, and the imaginatively amorous leopard slug (seriously, search "mating calls of the leopard slug" on youtube for an extraordinary BBC video) are the same forces that created you, too.

And we are each just a temporary experiment; elemental particles arranged precisely just so for a few thousand measures of a heartbeat before we, too, must surrender like our ancestor stars before us to the final dissolution and transformation of our essential nature.

Everything that pops into existence, even for a moment, clearly does so to offer its unique expression that can only emanate from that exact thing itself.

Only a rose can fully express "rose" with its infinite shades of undulating color, texture, and silky soft, delicate shapes of elegant petals perched atop a thorny thin stem. Likewise, only a goofy dog can fully express "goofy dog" and only a peach can fully express "peach" in all its sticky sweet succulence.

There is no other "you" on this planet. Your truth is the authentic voice of what your life form, your body, your heart, your being, the divine heavenly spark placed within you at birth, desires for in every moment.

Only you can fully express "you."

And YOU are a child of the Universe, descended from the stars.

Tell your truth already ... and let the peace fall where it may.

———————

A thought by Bryan Reeves

About the Author

A former US Air Force Captain turned Author / Coach / Speaker, Bryan Reeves has triumphed through multiple dark nights of the soul after hurling himself into the transformational fires of intimate relationship over and over again. With a Masters Degree in Human Relations and massive insight gleaned through countless adventures, Bryan now coaches men, women and couples in creating thriving lives and relationships. Bryan served on the Executive Council for the Global Alliance for Transformational Entertainment (GATE), and has worked on various projects featuring luminaries such as Marianne Williamson, Michael Beckwith, Deepak Chopra, The Oracle of Tibet, Don Miguel Ruiz and others. He is a regular blog contributor to The Good Men Project, Thought Catalog, Raw Attraction Magazine, Sexy Conscious Awake and more. He's the author of "The Sex, Flirting, Dating, Hunting and Hoping Diet" and "Tell The Truth, Let The Peace Fall Where It May." Connect with Bryan on Facebook (bryanreevesofficial) and his website (www.BryanReeves.com).

Thought Catalog, it's a website.

www.thoughtcatalog.com

Social

facebook.com/thoughtcatalog

twitter.com/thoughtcatalog

tumblr.com/thoughtcatalog

instagram.com/thoughtcatalog

Corporate

www.thought.is

22721688R00169

Printed in Great Britain
by Amazon